STOP OVERTHINKING ONCE AND FOR ALL

Techniques to Learn to Master Your Emotions and Overcome Negativity

Jun Sano

Copyright 2023 All rights reserved©.
No part of this book may be reproduced, duplicated or transmitted without the direct written permission of the author. In no event shall the publisher be held liable for any repair, damage or monetary loss due to the information contained herein, either directly or indirectly.

Legal Notice:
No part of the contents of this book may be modified, distributed, sold, used, quoted or paraphrased without the author's consent.

Disclaimer Notice:
The information contained herein is for educational and entertainment purposes only. No warranties of any kind are expressed or implied. Readers acknowledge that the author is not engaged in rendering legal, financial, medical or professional advice.

INDEX

Foreword	7
Gratitude creates happiness	13
Live here and now	19
Choose your battles wisely	25
The power of positivity	31
The energy of meditation	35
Don't compare yourself to anyone	41
What is the use of criticism and complaints?	47
Unconscious awareness	51
What raises your vibration?	59
The magic of equilibrium	65
Help yourself by helping	71
Too much pleasure creates pain	77
When less is more?	83
The secret of abundance	89
The benefit of being uncomfortable	93
The beauty of noninterpretation	97
The key to attraction	101
The ability to think less and feel more	107
Conclusion	111

FOREWORD

To begin with, I would like to warmly welcome you to this journey which, from now on, will be solely under your control. My sincere congratulations for having the guts to dedicate time and effort to your own personal development and to maintain your own inner calm. Those who have the courage to venture out of their safety zone and possess the ambition to follow their path are few, so congratulations. You are brave and have much to offer yourself and the people you love the most.

When we are faced with an excessive number of distractions, we are more prone to fall into the pattern of overthinking. In other words, when we fail to live in the here and now. Let's get this straight: what does this mean? If we think more than we feel, then we are not living in the moment; if we live in grief about the past or worry about the future, then we are overwhelmed by feelings of grief, anxiety, guilt, anger and resentment... and we think too much.

What is essential is that we realize as soon as possible that the human brain does not distinguish between real-world experiences and those that are only imagined. The feeling you get when something actually happens in your life is identical to the feeling you get when you anticipate what is going to happen. Therefore, you have to start taking that force into account so that you can use it to your advantage. The vast majority of our worries are unfounded or do not materialize to the extent that we fear they would. Therefore, instead of worrying about it, you must take action. Act instead of reacting to the situation.

When I say avoid reacting, of course, I mean reacting badly.

You may come to the conclusion that some chapters of this book have little to do with the problem of overthinking that the book primarily addresses. But each of them, in its own way, contributes directly to the calm and serenity you experience within yourself. They will also help you focus your attention on the here and now, gradually diminishing the mental chatter you experience and providing you with the balance and well-being you need.

Let me assure you that none of the ideas I will discuss with you in these pages are foreign to me. Through my own personal experience, out of necessity, curiosity and conscious choice, I have learned them all, assimilated, tested and ultimately incorporated them into my life because of the power they have and the wonderful results they produce. In addition, I continue to implement many of these strategies and secrets on a regular basis in my day-to-day life, as there is always something more I can improve or learn to make me feel happy and more grateful.

Believe me when I tell you that I would never be so dishonest as to provide you with something without first determining whether or not it is effective; after all, what good would it do you if I did that, just as what good would it do me? What good would it do me to expose to the world something that I'm not even sure is true or has any practical application?

If someone taught me something, I would have a moral obligation to pass that information on to the next person to ensure that the information does not become obsolete. If I have tried it and found it useful, it is only right that I share it. Similarly, there will be information that I have discovered on my own or that is someone else's method that I have versioned to suit me and, consequently, I adapt to it.

At least to some extent, most of these strategies or experiences are connected to each other and can complement or influence each other. When you have internalized and put into practice some of these insights, you will notice that your perspective has changed, that you are able to notice details that you had previously overlooked, and that what was previously unclear or incomprehensible about the world or yourself now seems crystalline and easy to understand or put into practice.

At that time, I could not understand some of the ideas that I can now explain with ease. I had not long begun my journey toward self-improvement, and I had a lot of material to assimilate. And, fortunately, I still have a lot to learn. But that's life, and it's such a brilliant teacher that if you don't learn a lesson, it will repeat it over and over and over and over and over again until you do. If you don't learn it the first time, it will keep testing you until you do.

The benefit of implementing any of these strategies or ideas into our daily routine is that as soon as we assimilate them and begin to apply them, we will see improvements in ourselves in relation to a variety of factors. For example, physical activity not only makes one healthier, but also helps the mind and spirit feel more enlivened. Practicing meditation not only helps relax the mind, but also lowers blood pressure, which in turn will improve circulation, concentration, positivity and other aspects of your life. And likewise, with each new chapter of this book, we have the opportunity to trigger a very powerful and beneficial ripple effect that will help us grow on all fronts.

Sincerity is the only thing that can forge a genuine connection between two hearts. This book connects my life with yours and serves as a bridge between us. One of the most effective and engaging forms of communication between people of different cultures. I will not be the one to question the longevity of that bridge or raise concerns about its possible future.

Therefore, I owe it to my word, my beliefs and my consistency to offer you material that you can share and use to further your own personal development.

When I came to the conclusion that this information was useful to me, that it worked well and that it helped me when I needed it, I became convinced that I should spread it to a larger number of people. On the other hand, as we all know, almost no one will let someone else help them until they expressly ask for it. It seems as if it is impolite to accept someone else's help. It would be almost the same as admitting that you could not solve it on your own, publicly confirming that you do not have the knowledge they want to give you, or stating that you need help, and of course, in the world we live in, admitting that you need help could be considered "weakness".

But, my good friend, the truth is that we are all more or less knowledgeable in a minimum of facts of life and totally uneducated in practically everything else. In other words, we are experts in practically nothing and students of everything. And why is it so hard for us to recognize this?

Out of pride, dignity, or concern for appearance? I don't know what the most popular explanation is, but it makes no sense to me why people do it. We all, and I repeat, we all, need or may need the right help at the right time. Do we seriously believe that the richest people in the world, who are considered the most "successful" guys on the globe, got to where they are entirely on their own and without the help of anyone else? No, sir, I don't think so.

Consequently, I believe that there are times when we need to let our guard down a little, at least when it comes to learning, let ourselves be affected by others, put aside our egos and listen to what others have to say. We must have the ability to listen without feeling the need to respond. To understand, you have to know how to listen. Put yourself in the place of the person who is speaking and try to understand what he or she has gone through.

And to progress and learn new things, we need to have a good dose of skepticism, not only about what we already know, but also about ourselves. Only in this way is development and progress of almost any kind possible. Thanks to the absorption of new knowledge that, combined with your DNA and the rest of your experiences and facts, will lead to the creation of new methods and a beneficial evolution of both your being and the world around you.

Have the courage to discover your optimal level of well-being. Your body will feel light and resilient, your energy will be fluid and overflowing, your attitude will be positive and joyful, and your life will feel different, full of happiness and abundance when you reach this ideal, maximum level.

Let's let ourselves go. Let's stop trying to be something we are not and let's be what we are. Let's surrender to our feelings and stop over-analyzing everything. At this very moment, there are no problems to point out. In this instant, there is complete and absolute stillness, and nothing bad takes place. When we already allow the mind to get involved, it fills the space with clutter. When this happens, it can be difficult to locate what is no longer in its place.

GRATITUDE CREATES HAPPINESS

Everyone has the ability to cultivate a feeling of gratitude towards others. It does not require a great deal of effort or investment of time, yet it has the potential to change our life and our view of it in a totally revolutionary way.

When we express gratitude for all that we have, we train our minds to be more aware of the blessings around us. We focus on the positive aspects. We are able to highlight the many good things that are happening in our lives right now.

That "what you focus your attention on is what you attract or extend in your life" is something that most of us have probably heard at some point in our lives. But I'm sure each and every one of us has heard the saying that "misfortune never comes alone". Isn't that funny? They are essentially the same thing viewed from two different perspectives. If I dwell on the negative, more negative things will happen. On the other hand, if I choose to focus on the positive, only pleasant things will happen. And if you or anyone else around you is really unable to recognize the positive things happening around you, you should take a deeper look. If not, try looking with different eyes.

We may have the impression that nothing pleasant is happening or that nothing great is happening right now that we are able to perceive. However, something special is happening. You are here. The mere fact that you are still alive is extraordinary in itself. The idea that you can breathe on your own is an intriguing topic of discussion. You are able to read these lines, you had breakfast this morning, you slept warmly, someone greeted you in the morning, you came home from work, you have money to cover your needs, you had a delicious dinner last night, you can walk using both feet, etc, etc, etc. Do you still believe that there is nothing that can be considered positive in your life?

There is no need for any of us to compare our lives with those of others. In fact, it's disgusting, as the proverb goes, but let's do it for the sake of simplifying a bit. How many people live in squalor all over the planet? How many suffer from hunger, cold, find themselves in the midst of conflict and other conditions? And despite all this, they have the broadest, most radiant smiles that are humanly imaginable on their lovely faces? Wow...definitely something to sit quietly and ponder. Who are we to judge between those who have "so little" and those who have "so much"? They laugh as they go barefoot in the mud, while we lament in our "castle". The Western world, sometimes referred to as the first world, struggles with problems such as depression, boredom and laziness. These problems are the result of excessive behavior. From an excess of joys that are superficial and fleeting, from an excess of stimuli that are meaningless and temporary, and from an excess of comfort. Both the creativity and growth of the human race are stifled by routine and comfort.

When we have more, we want even more. And the more we want, the less value we place on what we have.

It is not a question of not having sufficient resources. Or maybe it is. It all comes down to the value you place on what you have and who you are. It's not about getting everything you want; it's about wanting everything you already have.

When you are able to recognize the unlimited wealth that surrounds you, you will realize that everything is going according to plan. It is sufficient in every way. Everything that happens is a blessing, a fortune, a luck, a gift and a treasure. Almost nothing truly bad ever happens. And you are the lucky one who can tap into the wisdom of that statement. Take off the blindfold and stop thinking that others have "more" than you by comparing yourself to them. Check out the chapter titled "Pleasure for Pleasure's Sake" to learn why not everything that glitters is truly worth your time and effort. Not everyone who considers themselves wealthy lives a happy life. But by practicing gratitude, you can find happiness in life. You don't have to have a million dollars to be considered "rich." When you are sitting in the park and feel the sun on your face, you can feel the good fortune and the enormous abundance you have in your life. Or going for a walk with your pet on a Sunday while it's raining. Or go swimming in the ocean or a pool and experience how your body floats in a way defying the force of gravity.

Brother, what a joy to have you around at this time! The fact that we are here reflecting on this revitalizing topic provides a lovely feeling, don't you think? Tell your thoughts to take a breath and focus on the here and now; aren't there countless things you should be thankful for at this very moment? Then you should give thanks: to everything, including the universe, God, Buddha and Allah. To your own mother and your own father, as well as your own daughter or son and any brothers or sisters you have. To your next door neighbor, the baker and the person you work with. Whether you are alone or in company. Say it and experience the transformative power of gratitude. Notice how the universe immediately returns its energy to you when you feel grateful and the hairs on your body stand up as a result. This happens both when you express gratitude and when you make it known to others. And you do all this not only because you want to attract more positive experiences into your life, but also so that you can recognize and appreciate the many positive aspects in your life right now, without having to wait for them to arrive.

Exercise:

As soon as we get out of bed, let's get the body moving with a basic exercise. Find a place to sit and relax once you have refreshed yourself by drinking water and going to the bathroom or brushing your teeth. Put your hands over your heart and close your eyes. The right hand should be on top. Breathe deeply and calmly, and concentrate on feeling your body as you do so. Now is the time to give thanks for all that you desire, whatever you consider a source of blessing or good fortune in your life. Give thanks for your life, for food, for your home or job, for your family and friends, for your health; give thanks for growing as a person or for wanting to grow; give thanks for being generous or purposeful; give thanks for being sincere or sensitive; or simply give thanks for the desire to give thanks.

The immediate feeling should be one of extreme positivity. The powerful message that we are grateful for everything around us is transmitted to our entire organism, including the mind, body and soul. Every cell in our body receives the knowledge that we are healthy, joyful and surrounded by abundance. I repeat, this information is transmitted to every cell in our body. It is a beautiful thing that happens. In addition, this cycle has a self-sustaining positive feedback loop.

Do this exercise every day for the next month and pay attention to how your behavior changes, your attitude towards other people and how you react to difficulties or situations that might normally have a negative impact on you. I am sure it will allow you to see everything from a new perspective and reinforce your optimistic and courageous mindset.

This practice will transform the lens through which we view life and positively program your subconscious so that, over time, the thoughts that pass through our mind unconsciously and automatically become happier and happier and only reaffirm our happiness.

LIVE HERE AND NOW

"Stay present in the moment." "Carpe diem." "Make the most of the now." "Have fun with life." We've all been exposed to these marketing platitudes, but are we able to actually put them into practice?

We live in an age in which we are inundated with information and stimuli, in which there are hundreds, if not thousands of ways to obtain new "knowledge" immediately and from virtually anywhere in the world. This is the era in which we find ourselves.

But how should we feel about it? They say that too much of anything is bad and I agree that this is true in most situations. Personally, I believe that having access to an excessive amount of information is detrimental for two reasons:

First of all, no value is given to the information that is obtained, as it is excessive and is used in such a short time that it disappears in the blink of an eye. While we are working to finish processing it, we have already started to receive the next one.

Second, they completely disconnect us from the here and now. They are a constant source of distraction, and while advances in technology and information can bring us closer to loved ones who live far away, these advances can also make us feel more disconnected from those in our immediate proximity. By acting in this way, we remove ourselves from the present moment, which is the only thing that can truly be said to "belong to us."

Let's imagine for a moment that a child is born into a wealthy home. The family has a lot of money. Every year, on his birthday, on his name day and at Christmas, he receives a mountain of gifts of different sizes, colors and prices. No expense is spared. His parents want their child to have the best and to lack for nothing, or maybe they think it's a good way to raise their little one, surrounded by what seems like abundance, even if it's just material. In any case, they want their child to have the best and to lack for nothing.

Most of the time, the child will become a brat who doesn't know how to appreciate anything. Because he has been exposed to so many different stimuli and gifts, he quickly gets bored with them all. He has to constantly broaden his experience to maintain the joy he gets from doing things like receiving gifts or buying new shoes. It's all about hormones and the impact those hormones have on the human brain. That dopamine rush soon wears off and, after a while, you start to feel a void in your life, prompting you to seek out more and more stimuli so you don't have to reflect on what's going on. It is undeniable that this is an addiction, as well as a widespread problem in the modern world. In the section "Pleasure for pleasure's sake", we will delve deeper into this topic.

Let us now consider the scenario from the opposite point of view: a little girl who is born into a humble family that is on the edge of poverty, where everyone contributes to the household chores and where they consider themselves quite lucky if they are able to put food on the table once or twice a day for the whole month. The little girl loves to lend a hand to her mother and father. Since there is no TV at home, she spends her time chatting with her mother, reading and playing with her only doll, which is a bit worn out and no longer has the bow tied properly. Imagine the look on his face if, by a stroke of luck, his parents were able to save some money for his birthday and buy him a new doll. She'll be jumping for joy, running around the living room and hugging her parents while crying her eyes out and expressing her gratitude. This child is not accustomed to the excess of stimuli presented to her, so she does not live unconsciously, consuming without any sense of self-control. On the contrary, her mind is focused on the here and now and she lives in the moment without distractions or meaningless pleasures. As a result, she values highly the things she is given, the experiences she lives and the life she leads with her parents. This young woman has potential to become a good person who is content with having very little or even less.

The first case is exactly what happens to us in the here and now. We are subjected to such an amount of stimuli and such an abundance of information that comes to us through our cell phones, social networks, emails, calls, movies, series, work, news, press... that, for example, having dinner with our partner no longer makes sense or is of no use. And the fact is that we lead a life characterized by absent-mindedness, distraction, excess of meaningless stimuli, dopamine imbalance and living on autopilot. And, in fact, the things we don't see may be the most important.

If you are happy with your life, that will not benefit the big advertising corporations in the least. They are successful if you buy and use their goods and if those activities make you experience a momentary and ephemeral feeling of "happiness" or, more accurately, pleasure. But if you have a smile on your face, brother, a pair of torn clothes or an outdated cell phone can't take it away.

If you establish a solid foundation for your happiness, your life will be stable and meaningful and you will not need temporary or false motivations from external sources because you will have already established that foundation.

And you won't need the latest cell phone, the trendiest T-shirt, the fragrance worn by the famous actor or the car advertised on TV. You'll already be at peace and free of need. And, should you ever make the decision to buy any of those things, you will revel in them and value them for what they are: something ephemeral and material that in no way contributes to your sense of identity or influences the level of happiness you experience.

Exercise:

Touch the nearest wall if you find yourself distracted, upset or, especially, when bad ideas come into your head. As you do so, take a slow, deep breath. Now, direct your attention to what you are experiencing: is the wall warm or cold to the touch? Is the surface rough? When you place your hand on it, what do you feel? firmness? control? support?

And now, please tell me where is this bad idea or rage that has seized you.

It is an effective method to increase our mental capacity so that we are not corrupted by mental interference. It is a method to show you that there are certain things that the mind tends to do and that we must show it that we do not have the slightest intention of paying attention to it when it reminds us of them.

Think for a moment, do you think that the great men and women who have achieved success did it by listening to their worries, insecurities and negative thoughts? I don't think so.

Let's take a few moments to reflect on the following: now is the time when everything happens; now is the time when we can do something for our future; now is the time when we should do things that make us proud today and make us even prouder in the future. Be the director, the performer and the writer of the movie that is your life; don't wait for other people to tell you what it will be about.

CHOOSE YOUR BATTLES WISELY

There are many different ways for something to be misunderstood and there are many different possibilities for one thing or another to happen: maybe I didn't know how to explain myself as I wanted to, maybe I chose the wrong words or tone, or maybe the timing, looks or body language were not right. In addition, there is also room for error if the other person receives this message via a phone call, an email, a text message on their cell phone, etc. In other words, if they read it, it is logical that they tend to imagine how I would have expressed it and interpret it in their own way.

The other person may have had a difficult day, felt bad, and lacked the patience to stop and think about whether the comments meant one thing or another at the time. And because of the way your mind is constructed, as well as the knowledge you acquired growing up, it will help you interpret it in a positive or negative way.

It seems like it would be easier than it really is to reach a disagreement or misunderstanding based on personally interpreted differences, wouldn't it? Why, then, worry about being right? It is possible that neither is right - or maybe both are! Each read the words in their own way and, even if there was no ill intent on either side, a ridiculous misunderstanding may have been reached as a result. This makes it extremely relative and subjective.

There are numerous methods to know how to choose our "battles" or, more precisely, to avoid ego duels that lead nowhere; however, I rely entirely on Buddhist knowledge in this case, as in many others.

- **Do not take offenses personally:** it is not the other person's words that make you feel offended, but the other person's expression or attitude that makes you feel offended. It is you who "decides", consciously or unconsciously, to feel offended or angry. You get upset easily even for the most innocuous things. Because you don't agree, because it goes against your principles, because it is not the way you would do it or the way you want to see it, or because it conflicts with your ideas.

  Do not resist and do not allow the idea to provoke in you an unnecessary and possibly unjustifiable response. Accept it and ask yourself if it is really the way you perceive it or if there is even the slightest possibility that it could be something completely different while still being completely true.

  Don't make it personal, focus on staying calm and work to achieve inner peace. It is obvious that you should act whenever you can to avoid injustice and abuse. But, by taking offense, you are concentrating and intensifying the negative energy within you, making it last longer.

- **Abandon the need to win in everything you do:**

  What some people perceive as "losing," others see as an opportunity to grow. What some people consider "winning", others call "enjoying". If you let the desire to win affect you or transform you in any way, you will become someone cold and apathetic who only seeks victories and titles to puff out his chest and boast a beautifully adorned identity, but who is empty inside. If you don't let it affect or transform you, you will remain the same person who wants to win because it's a way for the ego to feel powerful.

We have all suffered victories and defeats, but is there a difference in the way we see the world? In fact, failure may even be more beneficial than success, since failure leaves you with a pleasant learning experience that you can cultivate, as long as you recognize that you are capable of learning something, as long as you are willing and as long as you are humble. But victory only fans the flames of the ego and sets you apart from others. What will happen if today's winner loses tomorrow? Will he feel depressed, irritated and have a negative self-concept? It doesn't make any sense. You are not defined by what you own, but by what you achieve, how you feel and how others make you feel. You are not defined by whether you win or lose; all you have to do is try to observe without judgment and enjoy life without trying to outdo anyone but yesterday's version of you.

- **Forget the desire to prove you are always right:**
When we are listening to someone, the vast majority of the time, we are actually preparing our response, we are accumulating ammunition to spew out our reasons or motives and we are trying to establish that our argument is the correct and sufficient one. This is how we protect the identity we have assumed for ourselves and express our desire to differentiate ourselves from others. However, we are already distinct from one another. We are equally distinct. But we strive to be accurate. We want to prove that we know better and that we are superior. But this endless battle is really ridiculous. I remind again that none of us is an expert in practically anything, rather we are all learners of everything. We all have a passing familiarity with various subjects, but our knowledge of other concepts ranges from scant to nonexistent.

By listening, without thinking about how to respond or, more precisely, by listening without thinking at all and simply perceiving the words, the attitude and the knowledge projected by the other person, we are allowing them to contribute something to us, to enter into us and enrich us with some of the knowledge they have acquired from their experiences. The variety of life is what makes it so interesting. And within the complexity of difference is the process of evolution.

I feel a surge of freedom as soon as I let go of the ego's limiting ideas and accept the possibility that there may be other truths than the ones I hold. I grow. I allow a new stream of ideas to enter my life and incorporate them into my life, which makes my life more vibrant and richer. Don't close yourself off to the flow of information that travels the Earth beyond your head and give yourself permission to question even your own identity at times, so that you can make room for other realities to coexist with you and interact with you.

- **Let go of the instinct to prove that you are better than others:**

We are used to, or rather addicted to, thinking that we are better than others. It is possible that this is the root of so many useless criticisms, jealousies and contempt directed against people who have more or less than us, those who are different from us and those who are similar to us. It doesn't matter; the important thing is to feel powerful. By despising others, I can avoid facing my anxieties, shortcomings and insecurities, which are the factors that lead me to seek my strength in impolite speech and behavior, to hide behind expensive vehicles and clothes, in jewelry and other empty vices.

You just have to be better than the day before; you just have to be a more evolved version of yourself. That's the only person you have to fight against to achieve your goal of winning. Period.

- **Free yourself from the desire to accumulate more stuff:**

To possess, possess, possess. To satiate our appetites, egos and desires to feel superior to others or to be included in a group. There are more beneficial methods to feel integrated in a group than just possessing everything that others have. If you consume yourself in vices and pleasures, you will end up burning out and lose your meaning and reason for being along the way. If you love money, you will always want more. If you seek one-night stands, you will never have enough and it will be difficult or impossible for you to value and maintain a stable relationship.

If you achieve one of your goals, you will immediately start planning the next one and end up wasting precious time that could be spent living, loving and learning instead of focusing on the next title or trophy to add to your collection.

The pursuit of happiness, rather than attaining it, is the real prize. It is more important to be than to have.

These are the principles of Buddhism that we will discuss today; however, there are many others that are just as interesting.

If we are not able to appreciate what we already have, acquiring more things will not bring us happiness; therefore, learning not to feel offended, forgetting our false need to be right, to win or to feel superior, and accepting that having more will not bring us freedom, are necessary steps to reach this goal. Free from the swaying of our ego, free from unconscious impulses that do us no good and free to know how to choose and select our conflicts effectively.

Have fun while learning these new skills and be sure to put them into practice to keep calm in your mind and in your life.

THE POWER OF POSITIVITY

They'll tell you, *"You have to have a positive attitude."* But sometimes it can be a challenge. Especially given the times we live in these days. That's why it is more necessary than ever that we learn to generate, feel and transmit positivity, and to have it as our primary attitude towards life, because it can benefit us in more than one and in more than ten situations every day.

Some things in life do not go according to plan. The results are not always as expected and, if they are beyond our control, the resulting repercussions are not always pleasant. At least, that's how we have become accustomed to perceiving things. But how many times have we heard that "every cloud has a silver lining"? And from my point of view, there is a lot of truth in that phrase, because many good things come after incidents that we judge as "bad".

Let's take an imaginary example: we have had a problem with our car. The fact that we have to pay the mechanic and that we have to find an alternative means of transport while it is being fixed is, of course, disappointing. If we want to get to work on time by public transport, we will have to get up a little earlier than usual. But if we don't lose heart and strive to maintain a positive attitude, maybe after dropping the car off at the garage, instead of rushing to the subway in a hurry or stress, you can enjoy the moment and relax. Maybe then you decide to "treat" yourself to breakfast at a coffee shop you've never been to before; and then suddenly you run into an old classmate you haven't talked to in years! You reminisce about old times, catch up, and out of the blue, you have the opportunity to collaborate together on a professional project. Wow! Amazing, isn't it? Good thing my car broke down.

Or let's look at another situation: you have been working in the same place for five years and, although today is a new day on the calendar, serving customers seems like a little torture: doing the same old operations, pronouncing almost the same old sentences... you are really bored or lacking in motivation... But if you get out of the loop you are in and pay a little attention to the present and make an effort to be nicer than usual, or ask the customer about his life or his day, everything will miraculously change for the better! Instantly, everything becomes much more interesting and enjoyable; you talk about everything, discover things you have in common, share some jokes and laugh, even if you don't even know each other! This may also introduce you to new people with whom you can strike up business relationships or friendships. And all of this is a direct result of making an effort to keep a cheerful attitude and focus on the here and now.

It is true that many thoughts arise spontaneously from our mind and that we have no influence over them, at least we cannot prevent them from arising. What we can do, however, is to decide whether or not to pay attention to those thoughts when they arise.

Exercise:
Ignore any negative thoughts or feelings that surface when you are aware that they are making their way through the thin veil that separates your subconscious and your conscious mind. Instead, focus on something else. Do some housework, sing, get some exercise, turn up the music and dance. I find it helps to hum. If my mind keeps mumbling unfavorable or discouraging things, I suddenly find myself singing a made-up tune or a familiar tune, it doesn't matter. *"Nana nana nana nana nana nana nana nana..."* and suddenly that negative thought disappears. It is no longer present. Because she is fed

up with you ignoring her, she has decided to leave. You have won in this case, but the conflict will not end here. The key difference is that you are now equipped with the right defense strategy to get out of the situation unscathed. Don't resist, accept completely and focus on feeling more by thinking less.

I pay minimal attention to what the mind has to say, but, if it can't offer me anything beneficial, I quickly shift my attention to something else, since I'm not interested in what it has to say. I smile politely and then write my to-do list for the day or start warming up for exercise. In the chapter "Present Contact," we will delve deeper into this idea.

Observe yourself every time you experience or rather believe something that is bad or does not bring anything beneficial to yourself or others. This is an additional strategy that can be used to re-educate thinking. Analyze it. If you have this feeling, you should ask yourself the following questions:

Exercise:

Why do I have this impression?

Do I really believe it, or is it just a meaningless outburst that has nothing to do with what I think or what I would like to do?

Is this an example of productive or destructive thinking?

Is it beneficial for me or others to develop this idea or take some kind of action in response to it?

And, perhaps most importantly for me: if I am witnessing the appearance of a thought, who exactly is it that is thinking it?

My view is that we make a major mistake when we confuse our mind with who we are as individuals. Our conscious awareness is under the control of our subconscious, and our subconscious, in turn, is under the control of the sum total of our life experiences and the knowledge we have learned. There are representations, ideas, laws and facts that are ingrained in our subconscious, although most of the time we are not aware that they are there. But they have a significant impact on how we behave, how we respond to things, how we evaluate what happens and how we live our lives. I think there is more than enough motivation to want to continue to do more research on the subject. Especially if we are aware that there is some unconscious and impulsive action or attitude that is not serving us or the people in our immediate environment. The time to educate ourselves could not be better. Be observant, analytical, accepting and open to practice in order to progress.

Or, to put it another way, every event we go through has the capacity to provide us with the education we need. But only if we stay alert. When we are calm and attentive, the universe unfolds before us and reveals to us all its limitless opportunities. And always keep in mind that a smile is the only thing through which all people on this earth can understand and communicate with each other.

Do you think it's a waste of time and energy to focus on being optimistic?

THE ENERGY OF MEDITATION

What do you think of the opportunity, power and strength you have to improve your well-being and health simply by changing the way you think? It's a wonderful idea, isn't it?

By practicing meditation we can relieve some of the stress and anxiety that comes with life. We forget the worries that haunt us, and when we are forced to face them again, we do so with a fresh perspective. We give ourselves the opportunity to re-establish the connection with our inner nature, which is the source of our serenity and sense of well-being."

The alterations that occur in our body as a result of meditation include:

- Decreased blood pressure, which translates into a greater sense of calm; and activation of specific regions of the brain that are associated with love, empathy and compassion.
- It helps us to be more coordinated and focused, as well as improve our memory and emotional stability.
- Relief of signs and symptoms of depression and anxiety.

There are now a large number of scientific studies that support the use of this type of practice. Scientists are now able to clearly identify the regions of the brain that are affected while meditating thanks to the development of brain scan tests. And the results are extremely satisfactory and promising in every way. Thus, there is already convincing evidence from the scientific community that meditating regularly gives us the ability to alter our thoughts positively. And to a great extent.

Other beneficial effects that can be attributed to regular meditation:
- It facilitates a more restful sleep.
- Relieves muscle tension.
- It reduces levels of the hormone cortisol, which is produced in response to stress and anxiety.
- By increasing the amount of oxygen in the body, the risk of developing cancer decreases.
- It facilitates the disconnection and relaxation of the mind.
- It has a positive impact on our overall health.

I strongly believe that we should start practicing meditation from an early age. Because not only on an individual level, but also on a collective scale, there would be drastic changes both in the quality of our lives and in the way we interact with each other. There is no doubt that civilization would make beneficial progress in its relationship with nature and pay more attention to the impact it has on the surrounding environment. We would probably take better care of ourselves, we would also eat more conscientiously, without inflicting such severe suffering on the billions of animals used in agriculture and industrialized processes for consumption.

And this would only be possible by setting aside a little time each day to sit quietly, focus on your own well-being and release any tension you may feel. Doesn't sound so difficult, does it?

The beginnings of meditation practice

No one is born with knowledge. At some point, we will have to start learning, just like everyone else. The learning process is an invaluable asset, as it helps us mature into better versions of ourselves and better prepares us for the experiences ahead.

Have fun with this unique experience that has the potential to provide you with many benefits that will help you improve your health and well-being in a completely natural way.

Sitting with your back straight and listening to relaxing music, preferably music without lyrics, is all it takes to achieve this. Enjoy the quiet moment you have created for yourself by breathing in slowly and deeply as you strive to feel more and think less. It's not about repressing your thoughts or feeling guilty for thinking, because those things come naturally. It's about being able to focus our attention on the music, our body or our breath when a thought comes to mind. Aromatherapy and the use of essential oils are two ways to help yourself at first.

In the following paragraphs, I will show you several different types of meditation for you to begin practicing:

Here are some different ways to meditate:

- Simply observe a photograph, a drawing or the wall itself. We can reach a state of relaxation and peace by breathing slowly and deeply.
- Mantras can be listened to or recited; in either case, keep in mind the following: energy is vibration and so is music. Listen to relaxing music or recite mantras and you will acquire the pleasant and serene energy you are looking for. This is one of the purposes of meditation: to raise our vibration.

- Breath concentration is the most frequently practiced or best known type of meditation, although most people find that they respond more favorably to a particular form of meditation. Feel the air coming in as you inhale and the air going out as you exhale. This is all you have to do. Concentrate your attention on the path the air takes as it enters and leaves your body, the sensation it gives you, or the calm it gives you.

Perseverance is the most decisive factor in any endeavor and seeing results is no exception to this rule. I promise you that, over time, you will witness tremendous improvements in the way you are and act and that these improvements will stay with you if you continue to practice.

These are some of the most fundamental approaches to meditation practice. But there are also other variations of them, as well as combinations of them; the important thing to remember is that, to practice any of them, you will need to have a quiet environment that is free of interruptions and to dedicate yourself to breathing deeply.

Begin a regular practice of meditation

- Practice a little on your own: do some research, get the idea and experiment with the different methods; you'll find it's fascinating.
- Reading a book or watching a video tutorial: living in the information age, you have a multitude of options to acquire the knowledge you are looking for; all you have to do is get down to work.

- You should seek the advice of a friend who is familiar with meditation; surely you know someone who meditates or someone who knows someone who meditates. There is no room for excuses if you want to achieve something.
- Sign up for a course: there are probably hundreds, if not thousands, of different meditation and mindfulness classes offered in different parts of your city. You can sign up for one of these classes today. Learn as much as you can and give it a try. You have a lot to gain and very little to lose.

Pranayama Meditation

I would like to show one of the meditations that I have found most useful and enjoyable when I started practicing. It is a form of Pranayama meditation. It is a fairly simple practice.

Exercise:
Relax your shoulders and keep your back straight while sitting cross-legged. As you breathe in gently through your nose, you should plug one of your nostrils. Now uncover that side and plug the nostril you were breathing in through. Exhale slowly through the side that has been uncovered and then, without any haste, breathe in again through the same side that you used to expel the air. Then cover it and expel the air on the opposite side. And so on.

Breathe slowly and deeply as you appreciate the peace and tranquility around you.

This type of breathing helps to balance the two hemispheres of our brain in a way similar to reciting the famous OM in a mantra. Thanks to this, it will be easier for us to maintain a healthy energetic balance and we will not have problems to enter into a deep state of relaxation.

Moving meditation practices

Over time you will notice that it is calmer, that you sleep better and that you find it easier not to get stressed. Or maybe you're no longer in such a rush to get to work and, as a result, you can enjoy the car ride or the music playing on the radio more.

Exercise is also a strategy that can be practiced at any time of the day and will help you relax your mind, reduce anxiety and stress, increase your ability to concentrate and improve your decision-making skills.

Feel your body, bring your attention to it, breathe deeply and concentrate on the sensation of the air entering you as you do so. Do this whenever you find yourself having negative thoughts, whether they come to you consciously or unconsciously. Pay close attention to the sensation in your arms, feet and the rest of your body as a whole.

And suddenly, the pessimistic thinking disappears. It is no longer there. You may have won this fight, but now you must prepare for the "war". That is, if you want peace. That's what they say, isn't it? I hope you have a wonderful day and are able to appreciate the priceless journey that is meditation. Peace.

DON'T COMPARE YOURSELF TO ANYONE

Comparing ourselves to others becomes very common for most of us from an early age. It is something that happens so often that we do it almost unconsciously and it is a behavioral inclination that does not really add anything positive to our lives or our levels of happiness.

You were the only student in your class who didn't have the trendiest toy, so you begged your parents to give it to you every chance you got. You had to be like them and have the same things they had; otherwise, you would experience the feeling of being different. Wow... Different! It's so hard to stand out from the crowd, isn't it? That's what we've believed all our lives, or more accurately, that's what we've been led to believe.

You were put in a math booster class if you were good in literature and languages, but not very good in math. This was done so that you would be at the same level as the other students and so that you would not differentiate yourself from them. That, however, makes no sense seen from my perspective. No matter how much someone tries to look like someone else, they will never be the same. There are a wide variety of forms of intelligence, and since the vast majority of us only possess some kind of intelligence in one area or another and not in all others, this highlights the fact that we are all unique. So why try so hard to look the same as everyone else? It is the most effective way to lose your identity and stifle creativity, to make you forget the talent and ability that life gave you in one field or another.

If your child is bad at math, but good at literature, don't just tutor him in math, tutor him in literature as well! In this way, he will be able to fully develop his potential in the area that sets him apart from others and that he is good at. If we act to resemble others, we run the risk of getting what they have and if we get what they had do you think that will complete you? If so, was that what you wanted to get or what the person you wanted to look like wanted?

If you act like someone you are not, you will attract things that are not compatible with who you are. You are more likely to attract things that fit your persona or mask rather than who you really are.

As young people, we are motivated to integrate, to feel that we are part of something and to interact with others. None of this is negative, except that we may end up losing our identity. Almost all of us, without even realizing it, build an armor that serves to protect us from the so-called "assaults" of the outside world. To hide any sign of vulnerability and avoid being an easy target, we clothe ourselves with an air of strength and insensitivity. It is unfortunate but true, this is true to a greater or lesser extent for everyone, depending on the region, the country and the conditions in which one has grown up. It is something that is rarely talked about and yet almost all of us do it. It is a type of emotional self-preservation, as well as a form of personal security.

If you reveal how you feel, they can use it against you; if you tell too much about yourself, they will envy you and judge you, etc. If you show how you feel, they can use it against you. People even ask for forgiveness when they cry during an event, meeting or other similar activity Why exactly do you need to ask for forgiveness, for being alive or feeling? It saddens me to think that a person would be ashamed to express that they feel or that they are "vulnerable" in any way. Crying or acknowledging your sensitivity does not make you weak, rather it makes you powerful and real, mature and aware, and I see nothing wrong with that. My point of view is that there is nothing wrong with expressing your sensitivity or crying. I, at least, have cried, cry and will cry no matter who is in front of me, if I am watching a movie or a documentary that has a scene that makes me feel something, whether it is a difficult or tender scene. I don't care if it's my wife or a whole movie theater full of people.

The ability to feel separates you from a world that can sometimes be hostile and cold. Feeling is pleasant, it is beautiful, it is human. It allows you to appreciate life from other points of view and to notice the small details that make the present great. But the most important thing is that feeling differentiates you from everything synthetic, artificial or cold that we sometimes relate to.

One of the most enriching experiences one can have is to feel in accord with one's unique personality, complete with all its virtues and abilities as well as its peculiarities. After taking off the shell, you will be able to see the world through your real eyes and you will be able to attract what suits your authentic self instead of what suits your shell.

Believe it or not, we are all weirdos and we are all as different as we are similar to each other. What exactly is this world's obsession with us behaving normally? It doesn't make any sense. If you spend your time and effort trying to be like everyone else, you will forget who you are. If you waste your life comparing yourself to other people, you won't be able to appreciate how much you've grown and how much you've learned along the way.

Also, one of the most effective methods to prevent happiness from taking root in your life is to constantly compare yourself to other people. Because you will be thinking about what that other person has that you don't have and maybe they got it in a different way and it probably means something completely different to them than it does to you. We are unique and we should not compare ourselves to anyone for the simple reason that no one is like us. We don't get the same upbringing or have the same parents, or the same DNA, or the same mentality, or the same way of seeing or doing things because we weren't born or raised by their standards. So why would I want what that other person has, out of greed or envy?

If that's what it takes for me to become someone else, so be it! However, you should strive to be a better version of yourself rather than imitating someone else's version.

Accept the parts of yourself that you cannot alter and work to improve the aspects that you can. And whatever it is that you admire about yourself, cultivate it, enhance it, expand it and make it your signature and your personal stamp. If you compare yourself to someone else, do it to gain something positive from the experience and not to envy them or feel bad about how things are going for you.

From my own experience, I am certain that, if one simply focuses on being oneself, one's relationships will be more authentic, one's friends will be more devoted and caring, and one's overall quality of life will improve dramatically.

A terrible fate awaits the person who mistakes his disguise for his genuine identity, his thought for his self and his ego for his self. We are, we do not think we are. Obviously, if I want to be one way or another and I do what is necessary to be, I will end up being; however, that is not what I want to express now. Rather, I want to say that we are more feeling than thinking, more being and giving than having, we live better when we live more in the now than in the past or the future, when we are more present than distracted. That is what I want to say.

Exercise:

The previous exercise, which is described in the chapter entitled "Criticism and Complaining," is comparable to this one. When you realize that you are mentally or vocally comparing yourself to another person, you should stop doing so immediately. Examine yourself carefully. Consider the motivation behind this perspective you have.

Maybe it's envy, jealousy or even simple annoyance. None of this is encouraging. Take a moment to pause and breathe. Take a look at your life and everything you've accomplished so far to realize how far you've come. You have a place to live, food, friends and health, plus probably much more... and with all that, you have more than most of our human brothers and sisters on earth have.

And are we going to be among those who do not know how to appreciate what they have? No. You must categorically refuse to let yourself be carried away by those thoughts that cannot bring you any benefit. Simply by the fact that you have come into this world you have already achieved success. You were selected out of hundreds of millions and traveled to the egg, where you created life together and eventually that life was born and became you.

You are great. You are wonderful whoever you are. I want you to repeat after me: "I AM GREAT". Once again, please repeat that phrase for me: "I AM GREAT". Now, with more gusto, repeat after me: "I AM GREAT". Go out there and achieve your goals. You are the master of your world.

WHAT IS THE USE OF CRITICISM AND COMPLAINTS?

"What a bad day!" "Stupid, look where you're going!" "That guy's a..." "I have to do it and I can't stand it." "I hate my job, but that's the way it is", etc., etc., etc., etc.

These comments and complaints, along with hundreds, or rather thousands of other criticisms and complaints, are what we are used to hearing or saying day after day. Even louder and with worse terms. In fact, there are well-known phrases and sayings that, for some inexplicable reason, contain more than one unfavorable word or phrase but are nevertheless ingrained in our culture.

They are a complete and total waste of time and effort. Literally.

If I spend even a small part of my time remembering how much I dislike my job, I will feel bad just for saying it, and I will feel that way from the moment I say it until the moment I leave the office or my job and stop working. And in the meantime, a mental memory will have been established in us that tells us things like "I don't like this," "it sucks," and "why am I not able to find something else?" as well as other arrogant or self-pitying and emotionally destructive expressions.

There are methods and means to deal with it, or more precisely, there are two ways to act: accept it or change it. While it is true that it is normal for something or many things to disturb us in our daily lives, there are methods and means to deal with it.

Why should I invest more time in my life in something that I cannot change and that I already know I don't like, if I already know I don't like it? Why should we express our disapproval with words? That will do nothing to alleviate our discomfort and, instead, will make the situation much more difficult to deal with. The work will become much longer and heavier, the hours will seem endless and the clock will tick even more slowly than usual.

It may seem that we are letting off steam and releasing ballast, but, in my opinion, what we are actually doing is reinforcing and consolidating that unpleasant feeling, giving it power over us and thus negatively affecting our energy, vitality and positivity.

Since what we express to the world through words has the potential to have a positive or negative effect on us, we must be mindful of the power of the words we choose to use. Let's not keep something in our lives that does not contribute to a positive mood for longer than is strictly necessary. We deserve better. You deserve better.

Still today, when I find myself in the middle of a complaint, instead of using a disqualifying or insulting adjective loaded with anger and in which I will invest a part of our time and energy that I will never get back, I shut up in mid-sentence or end it with "I don't like it". This is because I know that, if I say the qualifying adjective, it will be negative or unpleasant and will taint me and I want to avoid saying it.

Little by little we are indoctrinating our subconscious mind to the point where it begins to understand that we do not like to listen to complaints and criticisms, as they are meaningless and that we will not devote one more second of our life to them. By doing so, we will be in a position to put an end to the endless stream of negativity that has the potential to emerge on its own from our mind for no apparent reason.

Exercise:

When you realize you are about to issue a complaint or make a destructive criticism, stop your train of thought and refrain from speaking. Analyze it. Examine yourself carefully. Don't pass judgment, don't speak critically, and don't give authority over you to "evil" that has already occurred. Sing, hum, dance, do push-ups or just chat about the things you have to do today. Try to change the chip. Switch gears and think about something completely different. You shouldn't give that bad mood any ground to grow on in your day.

And, if you've already uttered that complaint, criticism or harsh phrase, it's best to change the subject and turn your attention elsewhere. You should not focus on it or try to make it better. Because, in the end, you will be the one who pays the consequences, even if the negative event was not your fault. And, even if you don't think or believe it, the choice will have been yours.

Although you have very little control over what happens around you, you do have a great deal of say in how those events "make you feel". Because it is you who makes the decision to experience those emotions. That's why I no longer use phrases like "that worries me", "you make me uncomfortable", etc. in my everyday conversations. Because I am the one who gets irritated, because I am the one who gets nervous, because I am the one who, unconsciously, let myself be carried away by that impulse and decide, automatically or not, to give in to that torrent of emotions and hormones that makes me feel strong after anger, confident after criticism and powerful after the rejection of the unknown. It is my decision and no one else's to feel this way or not.

This is the response we should have in determining whether or not to let a complaint or criticism about someone or something escape our lips and resonate in our being, modifying the vibration of the complaint or criticism and affecting us in a negative or positive way:

If we are going to criticize or complain about something, let us first ask ourselves the following questions: Is it true, is it good, is it necessary?

The vast majority of the time, if not always, harmful criticism, insults, complaints or victimhood are neither true, nor good, nor necessary.

Increase the amount of love you have for yourself and make sure that the only words you say to yourself are positive, inspiring and propelling you to be happier right now. Make the most of the power your words give you and refuse to let unfavorable thoughts, feelings or experiences alter the way you see things or diminish the likelihood that you will have a better life.

UNCONSCIOUS AWARENESS

Certain activities become natural to us and we carry them out without thinking. They are responses or impulses that occur below our awareness and do not require our authorization to alter our behavior. They wait in a hidden part of our mind for the right opportunity to arise, resulting in a response that is not always the one we expected to have.

It takes time to change an unconscious reaction, because it is part of the training we have received throughout our lives. This means that changing an unconscious reaction can be difficult. It is deeply ingrained in our consciousness and, as a result, we have been conditioned to respond in a certain way. In fact, this conditioning has been so effective that we already believe that the response is an integral part of our being.

Humans are creatures of habit and it is much more difficult to break an established pattern than to create a new one. It is also much easier to create a habit from scratch. For this reason, in the learning process it is always vital to unlearn rather than acquire new information. At the same time, however, it is also more difficult to understand.

It is a challenge to change our ideas and beliefs when they are based on something that has been established in us for a long time, because we are required to face ourselves and dismantle a whole structured system that contributes to the formation of our identity.

The person who adopted those beliefs yesterday is not the same person today. Even if we are quite similar, we will not be the same as we will be tomorrow. Consequently, everything we believed useful or valid the day before will not necessarily apply to us now.

This may provide us with sufficient reason to examine some of our behaviors, such as asking ourselves, "Do I want to remain the same person I was yesterday, who failed in certain situations, or do I want to continue living my life exactly as I am now in the present for the rest of my life?" Or do I prefer to learn everything there is to know about myself through trial and error so that I can be the best version of myself tomorrow?

To build solid and reliable happiness for the future, we need to work on it today, appreciate the circumstances we find ourselves in and have an attitude of gratitude. If we want to have a better physique in the future, we need to be fit now by exercising and eating right and we can't let our bad habits become routine. And this continues.

If there is something in the outside world that we do not like, we should first investigate the reasons behind our feelings. It is absolutely reasonable to feel indignant about something, at least to some extent, if it is something unfair or if we see someone being mistreated.

But if it's something more subjective, like the way your partner acts, or the multiple messages from someone who needs your help, or the way a car crosses your lane without posing a great risk to your safety and yet you still get angry or curse, yell or stay with discomfort inside, there is something inside you that you can improve today for your future well-being.

We do not begin to ask ourselves concrete questions until we become aware of the detrimental effects that certain unconscious habits have had, both in our own lives and in the lives of the people around us, and only then do we begin to investigate those effects. You are free to answer them in this space as an exercise if you wish.

Exercise:

Shouldn't I strive to modify my behavior if I know it negatively affects others or myself?

Is this an inappropriate response on my part, and why am I responding in this way?

Is it impatience, the fact that I want everything to be done the way I want it or the need to have absolute control over everything?

These types of questions can be really useful if what we really want is to get rid of an undesirable habit or routine. In this way, if we experience negative emotions such as anger or depression, we can turn inward to determine the source of the problem.

Because, in my opinion, when something "bothers" you, it is not that something that is the reason for your anger, but the way you perceive the situation. Sometimes, it is you and not the supposed problem, who has to change in order to find a solution to the problem.

You have no idea how many useless fights you could avoid if you would only pay attention to the fact that an impulsive reaction was going to come out of you at that moment. Then you can refuse to give in to it, save yourself discomfort by investigating your emotions or thoughts and thus perhaps come to the conclusion that the problem is not the problem itself, but how you interpret the situation.

And believe me when I tell you that each of us has at least one private problem to solve; from the perspective of those unaccustomed to dealing with our own kind of weirdness, we are all strangers.

Normality does not exist. At the very least, I have the impression that it is a legend. I think the most misguided issue is the aspiration to be normal or the act of pretending to be normal when, deep down, you are aware that, in doing so, you are denying who you really are.

Be weird. Be true to yourself. Don't edit what you say in any way. Nothing to lose, nothing to gain, but no filter. Jump for pleasure. Scream for joy. Run. Expect nothing in return for your generosity. Consume something delicious. Laugh out loud. Call someone you haven't seen in a while and let them know you miss them. It's important to express your grief, gratitude and affection more often. And never stop being thankful for the incredible good fortune of having friends who are still alive and kicking.

But let us return to the subject at hand. We want to change a negative aspect of ourselves that is detrimental to both ourselves and the people in our immediate environment. You have already made significant progress if you have recognized this unconscious behavior, emotion or impulse you have been having. Facing yourself and your shortcomings to create an improved version of yourself is a feat that only courageous human beings can accomplish. It can be difficult to face the mental structure you've relied on your entire life to function. But believe me when I tell you that, in this way, you can only get positive results. The real magic happens when you step out of your comfort zone and into the "positive discomfort" zone. This is the place where you will experience the most growth, where you will flow freely and with ease, and where you will discover who you are.

It seems a little strange that, in order to feel truly at peace, we have to go through some kind of discomfort first, but I don't think the idea is so strange or novel to us. For example, we have a sense of satisfaction after completing a strenuous workout, or after bringing a long-term project to fruition after working on it for months, or when we succeed in quitting smoking after struggling to do so for several years. It is a flash of perception in which we are fully aware and in the here and now, focusing all our energy on the experience of being fully present. After a lot of hard work and making some sacrifices, we have finally achieved something truly extraordinary. And it feels good, doesn't it? After achieving anything that requires a lot of hard work, there is a tremendous sense of accomplishment, happiness and relief that comes with it. After enduring a long period of "discomfort," we were finally able to make a major goal a reality; however, the sacrifice of that "discomfort" in exchange for a turning point in our life was well worth it. And all this is possible because you are here, in the moment, totally concentrated and focused on the present moment. Achieving incredible things one step at a time. Let us value and understand the genuine power of being more aware in our lives and being constructively "uncomfortable". This will allow us to live our lives more intentionally.

Exercise:
Consider whether, some aspects of yourself, such as your actions or reactions, are motivated by impulse or unconsciousness and have a detrimental impact on you or the people around you.

Stop talking as soon as you realize you've said something you didn't mean to say. Examine your own actions. Breathe in and out slowly twice. Answer the following questions on the paper in front of you: Why did I say or do that?

What did you hope to achieve by making that statement or taking those steps?

How do I feel about it, have I succeeded, was it really worth it to react that way?

If you have answered the questions honestly, you will be able to examine what happened from a new angle. Examine the impetus for your decision to respond the way you did. Is it genuine, or is it just the way you perceive it that makes you react that way? If we go inward when we feel that something is not right, we may realize that, most of the time, the problem was not on the outside, but in the way we interpreted what we saw on the outside.

Don't be angry with the person you are right now. You can accelerate the healing process and increase your motivation by saying out loud what you would like to hear, accepting yourself and taking care of yourself. You have responded according to the level of consciousness you possessed at that moment and that is all.

The only way to take control of your life and make it your own is to cultivate awareness. When you are conscious, it is you who draws your life; when you are not conscious, it is your life that draws you.

To begin with, we have to accept the fact that there is at least one aspect of ourselves that has room for growth. An imperfection, a negative attitude or anything else that does not contribute anything positive to the quality of our life. From that point on, we can separate the behavior or reaction in question from ourselves and understand what is going on. Even if we have not yet completed the task, at least we will have set it in motion. By doing so, we will create a kind of mental mark that will allow us to recognize that reaction the next time it occurs, which will allow us not to overlook it. Thanks to this, we will be able to anticipate the development of an attitude, action or mood that is excessive compared to what is required. Because, when it occurs, we will be able to recognize that this behavior does not correspond to us and we will be able to return to a mental attitude that is positive or neutral.

And so, as time goes by, this reaction will be limited until it reaches a point where it no longer occurs, because consciously, we have been positively programming the unconscious, making it understand that we do not like this reaction because it does not lead us anywhere and is of no use to us. There will come a time when we will realize that our immediate response to certain events is not the same as it was many months or even several years ago.

It is a process that involves perseverance, awareness and patience; however, the end result will be worthwhile and will significantly improve our quality of life.

In this section, list the ideas that have intrigued you the most so far:

_____
_____

How do you plan to put these ideas into practice in your daily life?

_____
_____

When you have finished writing these lines, you should read them aloud to begin to internalize them.

WHAT RAISES YOUR VIBRATION?

According to the fundamental principles of quantum physics, there is a constant transfer of energy between our body and the world around us. Therefore, it is best that we make sure that what surrounds us is good and positive so that the energy that reaches us is enriching and useful and also so that we do not run out of energy to use in our own development and evolution. If we do not take this precaution, we run the risk of running out of energy.

How many times have you just chatted with a wonderful friend and felt great, bursting with enthusiasm, appreciation and vitality? How often does this happen to you? This is not a random occurrence. It's more of a causal relationship. Or think about the other times when you've just finished a conversation with someone who is always negative, always criticizing others, always envying, insulting and belittling you every chance they get, and by the time you realize it, you're exhausted, depressed and don't feel like doing anything. I think we have all experienced something similar, but the question is whether or not we are aware of what is happening.

There are people who give to you and others who take from you; there are people with whom you exchange energy and others who leave you drained, dry and withered. On the other hand, there are other people in your life who can revitalize, strengthen and motivate you. We are energy and this fact cannot be disputed; however, sometimes, it is necessary to pay attention to these particularities to fully understand the notion, as well as the strength and influence it can have in our lives.

If we are energy and that energy is vibration at a certain frequency, we could say that the energy that makes up our body is in a state of high vibration or low vibration at a given moment. Each emotion is associated with a particular vibration, the positive ones have higher frequencies and the negative ones have lower frequencies.

There are many things that can influence our vibration, including the following:

- **Environment**: there may be more things in your immediate environment that influence you than you think. Maintaining order and cleanliness in your home or workplace not only makes it easier to find things, but also helps bring peace and quiet to your mind and soul and ensures that you are not absorbing chaotic energy from your surroundings.

  When we listen to music, its vibrations and energy can instantly raise or lower our own frequency, since, like us, music is made of vibrations and energy. When meditating or working, it can be helpful to tune into the right frequency by listening to upbeat, energetic or 432 Hz music.

- **Visual stimulation:** information sent from the retina to the brain through the ocular nerve is deposited in our subconscious, where it plants a seed that may or may not end up developing the desirable fruits we anticipate. We receive signals that remain in the unconscious part of our mind and tell us that we could have more and better, that what we have and what surrounds us is not the newest, the prettiest, the most expensive or the youngest. This happens when we see movies of violence, misfortunes or news that make you fearful and distrustful, or when we see advertising that motivates your consumerism and dissatisfaction with your current partner, house, car or physique. It may seem innocuous, but after years and years of being exposed to inconsistent information, our mind can start to play tricks on us and it can then become difficult to determine the source of your dissatisfaction. This is especially true if the factor that is causing your dissatisfaction has been deemed acceptable, as it is something we assimilate on a daily basis.

- **Company:** Some people believe that, on average, we are a reflection of the people who are closest to us. So let's make sure we are surrounded by positive influences. We have reached the stage where we can choose our own company; so let's make wise choices. Being surrounded by happy, grateful and optimistic people will make us feel better and bring more positive experiences into our lives. In contrast, negative people, who live their lives in a state of perpetual complaining and criticism and who constantly victimize themselves, will not help us attract anything positive into our lives and will only serve to attract more negative experiences. Make sensible decisions.

- **Words:** We should never, ever underestimate the tremendous power of words. Just as anything said to us can make us happy, sad or angry, the words we choose to say to others have the power to lift them up or bring them down. Words carry with them a potent charge of identity and intention that has the potential to move mountains and put every cell in our body to work with the energy we receive. This is why we often experience negative emotions simply by imagining something that hasn't even happened. This is due to the fact that the mind and the spoken word have a powerful influence on our body, mind and life itself. For this reason, I will repeat over and over again that destructive criticism and complaints are meaningless. This is due to the fact that even if the person or event in question is worthy of criticism, some of those negative words will splash back on us and contaminate our energy, resulting in a decrease in our vitality, positivity and overall effectiveness.

- **Ideas:** last but not least, we come to our ideas. The beginning of everything else. The basic material from which our most pleasant dreams or our worst nightmares can materialize and be experienced.

The crucial endeavor of "taking care" of our ideas is addressed in several ways throughout the various chapters contained in this book. Some of them are "Objective Interpretation", "Awareness of the Unconscious Part", "How to Be Positive" and "Feeling More and Thinking Less".

The human brain is a constant source of electrical impulses, which we call thoughts. And if everything in the cosmos is energy, think about what happens to those ingredients. They go out into the cosmos as a vibration with a frequency and then come back to you in the form of facts or justifications for you to keep thinking that way. It's a bit like the mirror effect, or like dropping a stone in water. The stone (or thought) will generate ripples that will spread out in all directions around the surrounding 360 degrees. These waves will become infinitesimally smaller and undetectable to humans, but they will continue until they complete their path. And, sooner or later, they will bounce back to the source, which is our existence, manifested in the language (high or low vibration) in which they were released.

Simply put, if you have negative thoughts and pay excessive attention to those negative thoughts on a regular basis, you will attract additional reasons, events and feelings into your life that will allow you to remain in that negative vibration. If, on the other hand, you make the decision to let go of those negative thoughts and focus your attention on the positive ones, practicing mindfulness and striving to live in the present moment with gratitude and love, then the positive events in your life will serve to validate the validity of that thought. It may sound like a theory or impossible, but I can attest that it is effective and, besides, what do you lose by trying?

THE MAGIC OF EQUILIBRIUM

There is a hierarchy that governs everything that exists on this planet. There are times when it seems disorderly, sometimes it seems meaningless or chaotic, but in the end, there is an order. Everything must operate according to a specific functionality, and if there is ever a disturbance of this balance, there will be a chain reaction of unfavorable effects. Humans, on the other hand, have the illusion that our lives are unaffected by or above this order. We believe that we are the masters of everything and that we are above it all, until everything passes over us. We are not immune to the laws that direct the workings of this cosmos. Let us not forget that we are not simply a part of the universe, but we ARE the universe. The same types of materials and compounds that make up the stars also make up our bodies. If we manage to modify our being, our dynamics, our attitude and our behavior, the environment will inevitably change.

But we fail to recognize our capacity for original thought. We live in a world that constantly bombards us with stimuli and distractions, feelings and addictions, all of which serve to obscure our perceptions and prevent us from realizing our full potential. We are the creators, the true creatives, and we are all or nothing. Naturally, we are linked to our environment, as energy connects everything and the energy that allows us to realize our goals in the physical world is our thoughts. Most of the time it comes into our heads out of nowhere, and although we may think we have a lot of control over what it says, there are cases where this is not the case. Finding ways to positively influence our "dreams" coming to life in the real world is a necessity for us and we must find those ways. We have to find ways to have a good influence on our subconscious to turn those negative, habitual, illogical and counterproductive thoughts into more pleasant, calm and logical thoughts. In the event that this does not happen, we will continue to limit ourselves from striving to fully develop both our potential and the goal or work we came here to complete.

The only way to make something work properly is to establish an order. The order is the algorithm, the formula, grandma's pie recipe.

You will be able to display all your talent and skill on the game board once you have found your order.

By order I don't mean that your apartment is clean and tidy, although it applies to that as well. If, according to quantum energy theory, energy flows from us to us and around us, an excessive number of misplaced objects will prevent the energy from flowing normally and prevent us from experiencing a renewal of our vitality and creativity. Aside from that, wouldn't it be true that simply perceiving how clean the space is would instantly calm the mind? Even though we have long been accustomed to seeing something cluttered, the instantaneous emotion that comes over us when we see it clean and tidy is one of serenity and restfulness, whether we want to see it or not. It's not a bad thing to have a messy room or kitchen from time to time, especially after a meal with friends or a day at work. On the other hand, it is not healthy to obsess about cleanliness all day long and suffer when we see a crumb of bread on the floor and lose our temper. Those of us who have pets know this phenomenon well. Simply put, and in my opinion, getting into the habit of cleaning up after yourself or not creating too much mess is really beneficial to your health and can be very calming. This is because it gives us a balanced place to relax and recharge our energies and ideas.

In the same way, you need to have order in your life, whether in your routines or in your activities, because this is the most effective approach to achieve what you have set out to do and reach your maximum level of productivity throughout the day, week and month?

Concerns that need your attention to balance your life

Many of us have some ingrained issues that act as an obstacle to our authentic progress. These issues can affect you.

In particular, I would like to draw attention to the following:

- Aversion to the unknown: when we make changes, as we "move away" from what we are used to, we may experience feelings of discomfort or rejection. However, stepping out of our comfort zone is one of the most effective methods to achieve our goals and succeed, if not the only one.
- You should avoid thinking or saying negative things about yourself, as a part of you will end up believing them, which will reduce your energy levels, efficiency, positivity and chances of success.
- If you don't want to do something, say so; if you don't want to go out for a drink that day, say so; if you can't or don't want to do something for some reason, don't do it. If you make sure you are healthy and take care of yourself, you will be able to take care of others without encountering difficulties.

- Putting off until tomorrow what can be done today: taking a break and doing "nothing" for a day is not only healthy, but also highly recommended. But if we let it become our routine, our way of being and our habit, we will waste priceless time that we can never get back and that we could have used to create, learn, work or achieve something.
- The main objective of this book: to avoid habits that lead to excessive levels of mental activity. One of the biggest keys to unlocking your true hidden potential is to reduce the amount you think and increase the amount you feel.

Exercise:

To jump-start the process of introducing new beneficial behaviors into your life, you should start by creating a calendar of events or plans. You can start with a manageable amount and then gradually increase it over the month so you don't feel rushed or overwhelmed. No doubt there is some activity you'd like to participate in, some book you'd like to read and some special dish you'd like to learn to make.

Fill your agenda, set yourself goals to improve and be open to new experiences. Because the only constant is the fact that everything is in perpetual change and this is the only thing that will never change.

Get a new notebook and fill it with your ideas. Write in big letters what you want to achieve. Leave one page free to jot down ideas, preliminary thoughts or drafts of strategies and budgets. Create a new to-do list on a new page each day. Be concrete, but don't get discouraged or overwhelmed if you don't achieve what you set out to do. Keep going. If you manage to complete most of the items on your daily to-do list, instead of beating yourself up for not completing all the items on the list, you should take pride in the fact that you've already accomplished more than you did the day before when you didn't use a list, notebook or starting point.

Keep in mind that if we want to include daily activities in our routine, it is easiest to start cautiously. Changes that occur gradually are preferable because they are more likely to be sustained over a longer period of time. In this way, we will not have the desire to give up.

Your program should include new tasks every seven to fifteen days. If you want to exercise more frequently, you should start by exercising only two or three days a week and gradually increase the number of exercise days every one to two weeks. This will allow your body and mind to get used to the increased demand and prevent you from getting discouraged and giving up.

If you put order in your life, you will be able to better appreciate the moments of leisure, rest and even work; in addition, your productivity will increase and the results will be immediately evident in your daily life and you will be able to work more efficiently.

HELP YOURSELF BY HELPING

When I was younger, I heard someone say that if everyone helped their neighbor, no one would need help. It seems to me that this says a lot about what we are capable of achieving if we learn to be more empathetic and sensitive, as well as learn to work more collectively than independently.

From a young age, we are instilled with the value of competing with others to achieve academic and athletic success, to acquire more desirable possessions, and so on. We spend our entire lives trying to classify ourselves into categories that we believe best describe who we are, but which, in my opinion, only serve to differentiate us from other individuals in our immediate environment. Indeed, there is such a thing as healthy competition; however, the reason it is not always practiced is because we tend to focus more on the things that divide us than on the things that unite us. Does the fact that a person "belongs" to something, such as a soccer team, a particular political ideology, a religion, a specific social class, gender or country, make them superior to those who do not "belong" to those classifications? Not at all. It only makes it different. And this is very positive. Take the natural world, for example, which is bursting with color and variety, as well as difference and vitality. That it possesses such a varied richness and abundance of things contributes to its overall appeal. Obviously, it's good to stand out from the crowd. In fact, I would go so far as to say that recognizing the innate quirks and characteristics of each of us and embracing them is not only necessary, it is what makes us free and powerful.

When we compare ourselves to other people and focus on the ways in which we are unique from them, we unintentionally build invisible barriers that separate us from them. As a result, we begin to view our uniqueness from a pessimistic or haughty perspective and close the door to our own growth, rather than being aware of the incredible educational opportunities available to us.

If we limit ourselves to socializing with people who are "similar" to us, we will not advance our knowledge much. It will be a fantastic opportunity to broaden our perspective and learn new things if we get together with people whose ages, ideologies, cultures, religions, countries or gender are different from ours.

Because of our unconscious rejection of the different and the unknown, as well as our deep "love" of comfort, I believe this is the main issue that contributes to our not having a natural tendency to be more open with other people. We do it automatically and frequently. And we don't have to travel far to notice it, or to locate a case of contrasts between nations, creeds or cultural practices. In the same nation, people who live in the capital may have a different attitude toward those who live in the suburbs, or those who live in the suburbs may have a different attitude toward those who live in the capital. Also people who live in one town may confront those in the next town and reject each other. It is unfortunate that this is still happening in the 21st century, but it does happen and the root of the problem is the fear of the unknown, the fear of not being in control of the situation and the fear of losing our traditions or beliefs. This limits the acquisition of new knowledge, which in turn slows down progress and stops evolutionary growth.

Don't give in to the temptation to let your mind direct your actions and don't pay attention to it if all it can offer you is doubt or anxiety. Follow both your heart and your natural instincts; this is the part of ourselves that we have neglected for so long but that is still there and compels us to try new things, take risks and continually educate ourselves.

It can be summarized as follows. Naturally, it is useful even without thinking about it. And if at first we have to make an effort because it is not easy for us, then let's force the machine to do what we want it to do. After all, it's all for a good cause. It may not seem like a big difference to you to help someone, but to the other person it can mean a lot. You've already improved their day or yours, and it's all thanks to a simple gesture on your part.

And by changing yourself, you contribute to improving the environment around you. It's the simple things in life that really make it all worthwhile. When combined with other "small" acts, seemingly small actions can have a significant impact.

There is no such thing as an unimportant act of kindness, nor is there such a thing as an unrewarding act of kindness. It is a fact that the positive energy and intention you put out into the world will, in one way or another, find its way back to you, whether at a greater or lesser level. As a result, the cycle of humanity, which is made up of empathy and fellowship, will run its course and will never be lost. Let us participate in making the world a better place for others and embrace only kindness and goodwill in our immediate environment. By doing things this way, we will establish our own world and our own laws.

Be careful not to lose sight of the sun because of the storm. And remember to be someone's ray of sunshine today. Be the one who makes a difference, be the one who surprises and makes others doubt the injustice of today's world and be the one who restores hope in humanity in these modern times by being the one who does good selflessly. "For no apparent reason", without purpose or party and without fear of divine punishment for not acting "properly", let us spread a little fantasy, joy, affection and good manners on the ground on which our human family walks. Let's do it "for no apparent reason". Let's do it because it's the right thing to do, because being kind to others makes good things happen, and because helping our equals is an absolute necessity, and by equals, I mean different, and by different, I mean equal. Let us help each and every individual who crosses our path, whenever we see that we can help them or improve their lives with a simple smile, a kind word, a genuine interest or a detail. Let us do so whenever we perceive that we can help or improve their lives with any of these things. It is a seed that will grow the tree of humanity and will bear only fruits of understanding, respect, companionship and love. No symbol of affection falls on deaf ears as it is a seed that grows the tree of humanity.

Exercise

Be aware of your day to day life. There is someone around you whose morning or evening can be made better by the help you can give them. Maybe it's giving them a smile, helping them push their car, or holding the door for them. Don't pass up the opportunity to temporarily step out of your comfort zone and help someone else today. You will brighten that person's day and you will have moved closer to the idea that we are all equal and deserve equal love, respect and opportunity. Smile at the person you think doesn't deserve it as much as you do and also at the one who does. Your generosity should amaze everyone you come in contact with.

In the end, you will have forgotten your everyday problems, troubles and worries by concentrating on the well-being of others, which you will have achieved without even recognizing it. And you can't put a price on that.

TOO MUCH PLEASURE CREATES PAIN

How incredibly tasty the cuisine is and how much we love sweets. Or how much we enjoy having satisfying sexual encounters, smoking, shopping, earning and spending money. Or how nice it is to have a beer sitting on a terrace in the middle of summer.

The vast majority of these habits or activities are not at all harmful. In fact, "indulging" in the occasional "luxury" of having a beer while chatting with friends or something similar is not only recommended, but considered healthy.

No one is going to take care of you as well as you do, so don't expect anyone else to. It is very beneficial to engage in self-care and make time for quiet reflection and relaxation; in fact, we should do it not only as a reward for our efforts, but also for the sheer pleasure of doing it. For our purpose in this life is not just to work and work, to busy ourselves and worry about our duties and bills and pay the bills we owe. It is to stop the train at intervals, to disembark, to breathe some fresh air and experience the gentle warmth of the sun on our faces. Try to feel more and think less. However, that is by no means the whole point.

When I talk about pleasure for pleasure's sake, I mean basing your happiness solely on your ability to experience pleasurable things. That is, thinking that you are happy because you have more money, more sex, because you feel superior to someone else or because you have spent it on frivolous or unnecessary things; or because you have earned more and more money.... That is the real mistake and, in fact, it is a real addiction and very dangerous for our mental and emotional health.

Because there will come a time when you will have done everything, or almost everything and you will feel empty, unsatisfied, depressed and irascible, you will take it out on yourself or your loved ones and you will try to drown your sorrows in alcohol, overeating, drugs, sex, etc.... And, with that, we are back to square one.

One of my best friends is a millionaire. And, fortunately, he is the optimistic, grateful and happy type of person. However, he reveals to me that many of his friends, who are also millionaires, are addicted to sex, alcohol, cocaine or prostitution or are lonely and depressed.

This is because in their minds they confuse pleasure with happiness. It can be summed up in a single sentence, but the concept behind it can be difficult to understand. I will make an effort to describe it in a more understandable way: pleasure is an external stimulus that gives us a pleasant feeling of well-being, a source of hormones that flood our organism and revolutionize it. Pleasure originates from the outside, it is a stimulus that comes from outside. Whether it is the consumption of unhealthy foods containing flavor enhancers, processed sugar and other artificial additives, the acquisition of wealth, narcotics, political power or sexual activity. The feeling of pleasure is not something that can be sustained. It comes, fills us momentarily and then fades, leaving behind only a vague memory of how wonderful it was while it lasted. Afterwards, we need another dose to satisfy our parched throats. It's a never-ending story.

Happiness, on the other hand, is an internal state that cannot be bought. It is a state of mind and a way of life. It's not so much where you end up as how you get there. Even if it's pouring rain outside, your insides can feel like a nice, sunny day. We don't need anything physical to experience joy; rather, it is the lens through which we view the world that determines our level of contentment. We don't have to sit and wait for the storm to pass, but learn to move gracefully in the rain.

People often suggest that thankfulness is a trait shared by happy people, but I don't see it that way. My theory is that happy people are those who are grateful for what they have. Because if we give importance to what we have, how we feel and who we are, everything else in our environment will take on a different hue. When our work schedule is changed, we will focus on what we can do by having a different shift, like that pending task we wanted to do; or if we have to work more, we can think that we will earn more money if we work more hours and what we can invest it in, etc. A rainy day will feel good to us because we will be at home warm or in good company.

As explained in the section "Being grateful makes you happy", if we are aware of the abundance that surrounds us and the privileges we possess, we will, of course, experience extraordinary happiness.

When I mentioned that happiness comes from within and pleasure comes from without, I was referring to this very concept. When we keep in mind how fortunate we are, when we value our health, our life, friendships or family relationships; when we appreciate the love of our partner or our pet, when we enjoy a sunny or rainy day, when we are grateful to have a roof over our heads, a plate on the table, a job, good conversations or company, and a long etcetera, then we will not need an external stimulus to feel happy. Because the feeling of inner calm and gratitude we will have will be so powerful, this experience will take our energies to a new level and our perspective of the outside world will change as a result. Each of us will see the same sky from our own perspective. We will walk in a different order on the same path. The world as we know it will still exist, but our species will have progressed. Suddenly, our worries will be fewer, our problems less severe, our anger will diminish until it disappears altogether, and smiles will become our new language.

As we will have realized that the secret is not to acquire but simply to be, happiness will come to us easily and almost unintentionally. This is because we will no longer focus on material possessions. Even in those times when you seem to be doing poorly and have a rough patch, when multiple difficulties or anxieties come together, even then, there is surely much to be grateful for. At the end of the day, it all comes down to being happy and making the people around us happy.

Exercise:

It's easy, I recommend that we write down on paper everything that we know does not do us any good, neither to our physical health nor to our mental or emotional well-being, and yet we continue to give it a place in our lives. Take it out of you, make it part of the world around you and make an effort to see it in an isolated or more objective way.

Write down directly those things that give you pleasure but that you know will not do your mental, emotional or physical health any good in the long run.

Let's give direct answers to these questions:

What am I achieving with these bad habits or these excessive amounts?

Doing so gives me joy, but does it also make me happier? Does it also make me a better person?

If I stopped doing it, what do you think would happen?

How can I receive the same sensation it provides me by safer and more natural means, or how can I acquire an even better sensation for my health that lasts longer?

If so, why don't I choose that option?

Now write down, on the same paper, the things that bring you true happiness and that do not put your mental, emotional or physical health at risk.

Answer this question:

Is it possible that most of the "things" that make you happy are not "things"?

It is not my place to judge you. I have been there and it is my intention to guide you through the steps I followed that worked for me to stop being a slave to the mind, the negative impulses and the unconsciousness that rules almost all of us to a large extent.

No one but you will see your answers, so it is important that you strive to be as honest as possible. This will allow you to identify as soon as possible the origin of the "problem", which is not such, but a concrete fact caused by distraction or unconsciousness.

You may also choose to discuss this information with your partner or other loved ones, who will be able to help you in the search for tangible evidence, thus making the process easier and more pleasant for you.

It is very important that we take time out of our lives to free ourselves from the burden we feel we have to bear alone and to communicate how we feel to the people closest to us. In this way, we manage to externalize the "issue" and, in doing so, everything is relativized and, to a certain extent, loses its importance.

Let go of any feelings of shame, pride or fear and bring out whatever it is that is hiding inside of you that is holding you back.

Emptying your backpack of stones is very healthy and beneficial for everyone. In addition to this, you will realize that you may not have accumulated so many and, as a result, you may rethink your decision to do so in the future.

WHEN LESS IS MORE?

From a very young age, our brains are flooded with advertising for cars, beautiful people, colognes and more beautiful people, among other things. These are visual stimuli that, as we discussed in the chapter entitled "High Frequency", are progressively deposited in our subconscious, changing the nature of our mind and making us hungry to consume, alter, buy, throw away... and buy again. This is due to the way our mind works. Don't get me wrong. It's always a good idea to be open to new experiences and opportunities, especially if you're not happy with who you are or where you are right now. But if you seem to have it "all", there will come a time when you give in to routine and boredom, or you become demotivated and stop recognizing and appreciating all the wonderful things around you. Then, in an effort to regain that feeling of freshness and enthusiasm, you may make the decision to give up everything you have worked so hard to achieve in recent years and start from scratch. You give up what you love and what you've had for so long in order to have for a brief moment what you "want" or, more accurately, what you think you want. And it's all due to the incessant bombardment of stimuli that feed your already existing feelings of dissatisfaction and stir up your already present anxiety. That's the kind of change I was referring to, although I think it's more accurate to speak of involution than change.

Furthermore, in the chapter entitled "Pleasure for Pleasure's Sake," we talk about how essential it is to avoid basing our "happiness" on fleeting and superficial pleasures. This is because we will always depend on an external source to feel that momentary "well-being" that pleasure provides.

Once again, I want to make it clear that indulging in pleasure is not inherently sinful, as long as we do not let it control our lives or become an object of abuse or obsession. Everyone fits in well on a moderately frequent basis with sexual activity, alcoholic beverages or shopping. However, if we turn something that can provide momentary relief in some circumstances into the only source of relief in our lives, there will come a time when it will provide the opposite effect. One day, our so-called "well-being" will consist entirely of our body and we will feel depressed, empty and unmotivated inside.

I have personal experience with people who were born into wealthy families but who, by the age of 30, were suffering from depression, alcoholism or other serious vices.

Let us reflect on these words, because I believe they represent a very significant piece of advice:

A road that leads nowhere is paved with overstimulation and, more specifically, with the fixation or desire to acquire more and more material things. Or, more accurately, it leads nowhere worthwhile. If we strive to acquire more and more things, we will end up seeing nothing of value. And if we keep going around looking for stars, we will end up losing sight of the moon.

It's not about having the mindset that we have less stuff, it's about having the mindset that we have everything.

Even if we continue to desire something else or want to achieve more goals, we must always be grateful so that we do not forget where we come from and the great abundance that surrounds us and of which we are a part on a daily basis.

There will always be someone with less than us who is content with their life and there will always be someone with more than us who is miserable. Therefore, we should be aware of how fortunate we are simply to be here and now, reading this book, in a private moment of calm and inner search, investigating, evolving and acquiring a greater understanding about this wonderful and complex mechanism in which we have been granted to live, our being.

If we knew all the tricks, there would be no more fun; if everything were easy, it would be boring; if we had all the riches in the world, a different "love" every night, and all the money, sex and vices one could dream of, nothing would be worthwhile. Nothing would be worth the time, work and sacrifice it requires, not to mention the necessary willpower. How could we then place a value on it?

There is a proverb that says: "Easy come, easy go". It can also be interpreted to mean that what was easy to achieve, whether it was easier than expected or not, will eventually disappear. If we did not have to make any effort or sacrifice, if it was not "hard", if we did not have to concentrate and pay attention, if we did not have to give up our free time to achieve it, then it will mean practically nothing. A mental marker will be placed in our head as if to say: "Ha, I got it quickly and easily, I can have it whenever I want and there will be many more like it". Then you will believe that, if it doesn't work for you, you can take another and another without stopping to appreciate the experience or value anything and you will continue to believe this even if it doesn't work for you.

I came to the conclusion that a chapter with the title "Sometimes Less Is More" would be beneficial for several reasons, including this one. Although it may seem like a simple idea that can be summed up in a few sentences, many people find it difficult to assimilate.

"Less is more" does not mean believing that you have too little, but having the attitude that what you have is enough; it means being grateful for who you are and what you have; it means being aware of the abundance of love and beauty that surrounds us.

That is why I use the word "think" when I write "think you have little", and that is why I use the word "feel" when I write "feel that what you have is enough", because thinking does not have to imply awareness on your part; we all think every day without having to be part of that "action" and most of the time thinking happens without us having to do anything at all. That's why I use the word "feel" when I write "feel that what you have is enough." Because emotion is a completely different matter. Even if we don't perceive it that way, most of the time when we feel we are making a decision, even if we don't realize it. First I think, whether consciously or unconsciously. Then comes the feeling and then the sensation. It takes more participation on our part to feel than to think.

If a thought occurs to us out of nowhere and we give it our full attention for a predetermined amount of time, we make a conscious decision to feel a certain way and this gives rise to a feeling that can be positive or negative, depending on the nature of the thought and the degree to which we can visualize it.

Exercise:

Look at everything in your life: do you have a home, a family, a job, friends, a partner, do you eat more than once a day, are you healthy, do you have free time, can you exercise, read or go to a new restaurant? Do you eat more than once a day? Do you have a partner? Then you have access to much more than 75% of the entire population.

Take a deep breath and softly say out loud *"I am grateful for this moment and the experience I am receiving"* as you feel the power of the words of gratitude you are reading. Thank you.

Repeat these words aloud: "*I am fortunate because I have a home, food, health, work, friends and love. As a result of my great fortune and the fact that I am surrounded by abundance, I don't need anything else to be happy. Happiness has already found me. I lead a good life.*

As I breathe deeply and slowly, a smile comes across my face. In addition, I do everything I can to ensure the happiness of those around me.

Thank you very much, world. Thank you air. I thank the radiant sun. I thank life.

I wish wholeheartedly for the power of these words to resonate in you and permeate your being. Keep in mind that you can reinforce something in your mind by repeating these affirmations whenever you want, as well as others that you develop yourself, in order to strengthen something. The power lies not only in the words themselves, but also in the meaning they convey and the perspective from which they are read.

You have a lot of power. One of the many ways in which your mind possesses the ability to bring you inner calm and contentment is the one you have just realized. Never forget the power you possess.

We enjoy a privileged position. As I said before, sadness and boredom are more common issues in the first world, or in the West. Only here we are so easily sidetracked by so many external stimuli that we are unable to stop for a few minutes and breathe slowly and deeply to feel our body, train our mind to slow down and nurture our own sense of serenity.

THE SECRET OF ABUNDANCE

The concept of abundance can sound like having a lot of money, living a luxurious lifestyle and splurging. However, it is also a spiritual term that can be used to describe all the positive things that come to us and are around us. Realizing that we have been blessed leads to feelings of gratitude, having those feelings of gratitude leads to feelings of well-being and having those feelings of happiness is the secret to having abundance.

Since not as much happens in nature as in the city, city people may consider being in the middle of nature to be uninteresting. On the other hand, being in a mountain can be an absolutely mind-blowing adventure for another person who comes from the same village, the same neighborhood or even the same family as you. The same place of birth, a very identical DNA? what's different? The eyes that assimilate the landscape and the angle of vision.

Whatever we pay attention to grows in our lives. If we focus on the negative, we are sending the message to the world that we take pleasure in the negative, which will result in the manifestation of more negative events. On the other hand, if we choose to think positive and appreciate all that makes us who we are and all that surrounds us, we will experience a life full of abundance.

If I take a walk in the park, I may find myself thinking about the stressful events of the previous day at work, about how little I want to show up the next day and how much time I have left to complete that arduous task.... And, suddenly, something unpleasant happens to us; either we step in a dog excrement, or we get a scare when crossing the street because we didn't pay attention and didn't look before crossing, or the phone rings and someone communicates unpleasant information. Since when does one horrible thing happen to you and then it seems that another one follows right behind it, and then another one, and then another one...? However, this is not the case, it is because our internal filter causes us to focus only on the negative aspects of the situation, ignoring any and all positive aspects.

Possibly, if we had not been so preoccupied with our own thoughts as we strolled through the park, we might have noticed what a wonderful day it was, or those curious flowers that had grown on the side of the road, or that little girl playing with her dog and dying with laughter every time he returned her ball. These are all things we could have stopped to appreciate if we hadn't been so preoccupied with our own thoughts.

What you want to see is what life is. It is a combination of unforeseen events that are precisely arranged along with your perspective and your way of seeing things in the world.

They say attitude is everything, and these people are not wrong in the least. One person may find a certain event tedious or unappealing, while another may find it fascinating and intensely enjoyable. Yes, we are all unique. However, if I am unable to recognize, appreciate and express gratitude for the tremendous richness that surrounds me, shouldn't I make an effort to modify my thinking so that I can do so?

What some consider leftovers, others consider food. What may be an unpleasant experience for you may be an opportunity for growth for someone else. Some people's idea of hell is someone else's idea of work and willpower. And if, after reading these lines, you are still unable to recognize the abundance that surrounds you, as other people do, then maybe you should be someone else. Change yourself. Meditate, grow, educate yourself and transform your being. Adopt another role. Be the person you imagine yourself to be.

The person who finds pleasure in a cloudy day as much as in a sunny day, the person who can put a smile on the face of someone who is having a bad day and make their day better. Be that person who offers help without expecting to receive anything in return. If you know who you would like to become and have not yet done so, you should get to work right away, because there is less and less time left to understand. Every day moments, adventures, feelings, laughter, friendships and life itself slip away. Someone else will live it in your place if you are not here to do it. But it won't be you, it will be someone else. If you can't laugh out loud for no reason, if you can't smile at a stranger, then be someone else. If you don't like this day, no matter what it's like, if you're sick of your job and you're still in it, then be someone else.

There is much available in all forms and environments. It is sustenance; it is fuel; it is energy; it is love; it is melody; it is joy; it is life. It's when you meet someone for the first time and immediately feel like you've known them before because of their wonderful chatter. It's like you're strolling down an unfamiliar street and suddenly you see a restaurant serving cuisine from another culture and decide to go in to try unusual flavors. It's when you discover a new singer and instantly fall in love with virtually all of their songs. When you visit a foreign nation for the first time and discover that you have a tremendously positive impression of the culture and feel that you would like to live there. If you have felt something similar, then you have experienced abundance. But none of this will happen if you are unable to appreciate the abundance before you and if all you see in the sky are gloomy clouds. There are times when things don't even exist and yet we make them up. Especially because we think, act and materialize. Therefore, we are, to a certain extent, the creators of the reality we experience. In school we were never taught to design our lives or write our destinies, but it is never too late to acquire new skills; learning is something you can do at any time in your life.

Exercise:

When you leave work or at the end of the day, go home and find a comfortable place to sit. Take a few slow, deep breaths to calm yourself. Take a moment to open your journal or notebook and write down the current date. Write down two positive experiences you have had today, whether they are words that other people have said to you or feelings you have had, things that have happened to you or that you have noticed. Something fresh and uplifting. If you feel confident, write more, as many as you want. Now read them again, what feeling do they give you?

Repeat this exercise every day for a month. In this way, we are educating the mind to focus on the good in our life. In this way we eliminate negativity and depression or dissatisfaction. In doing so, we cultivate awareness of the unlimited abundance that surrounds us and of which we are a part in every moment of our lives.

THE BENEFIT OF BEING UNCOMFORTABLE

After becoming aware of the importance of stepping out of the comfort zone, this idea became deeply ingrained in my mind. Or, to put it another way, instead of sitting around waiting for the right opportunity to arise, you have to act, seize the moment and make it the right one.

We know very well that we are creatures of routine and that, when we get home, we prefer to take off our slippers, have a drink, have dinner, read a book or watch a movie, depending on what we feel like at that moment. It is a method to feel at peace and there is nothing terrible about it, at least when it is in the right balance. We feel safe and comfortable in our home and in the tranquility that the habit gives us.

However, if maintaining that comfortable habit prevents us from working on ourselves, taking risks on new projects or creating new connections, or engaging in a variety of activities to gain a breadth of experiences, then it may not be especially beneficial.

To a certain extent, comfort is positive, but if we want to develop as individuals or entrepreneurs, abusing the benefits of comfort can be extremely destructive to our efforts and future.

It goes without saying that we all like to feel comfortable at home or with some circumstance, activity or undertaking that we have already mastered. The will to want to improve, on the other hand, or the drive to reach our limit and then surpass it, is something very positive and satisfying.

We have to accept that the vast majority of the information we know comes from experience and, more specifically, from unpleasant situations, as this is when we learn the most.

Fun and education can be found in all aspects of life; therefore, there is no reason not to make good use of this information. Let's aim to fail often. I am not suggesting that you fail on purpose, but you should try new ideas, try new projects, fail, learn and adapt.

People who have achieved great success often talk about the value of setbacks, or the "failures" that the rest of us tend to view with such disdain. However, they are not the same thing. They present wonderful possibilities for education, advancement and the pursuit of one's goals. It's safe to say that almost no one gets it right the first time they try, so just having the opportunity to do it again is a privilege. Now that we've had a moment to catch our breath, let's think about how we can make the next attempt even better and then give it our all.

Consider the following scenario as a concrete illustration of what to do when you want to go to the gym or exercise:

When we go to sleep the night before, we motivate ourselves and convince ourselves that this is what we want to achieve, we think about starting the next day or the week at full speed and, when we wake up, we say to ourselves: "I can do this! When it comes down to it, we find a thousand and one persuasive excuses not to do it because we are lazy, something hurts, or something else.

It no longer seems like a choice you can make, but a duty you have to fulfill. And, if you think about it, that ruins the whole experience, doesn't it?

Even when doing something that requires little effort, gives us great satisfaction and makes us feel positive and fulfilled, we find it extremely difficult to turn off the thoughts running through our heads, get off the couch where we are safe and engage in an activity that we find rewarding. But I believe that doing something different or stepping out of our comfort zone is what drives us to turn it down in the first place.

We may find it hard to go for a workout. But once we are in the middle of the workout, five to ten minutes after we start, we have a fantastic feeling, our mind is calm and stress-free, we can feel the blood circulating throughout the body, giving it energy and when the workout is over, we feel like winners!

Exercise:
Think about the activities you usually do throughout the day, but do reluctantly or because you lack enthusiasm for them. Let's adjust that perspective and mindset so you can approach them with enthusiasm and positive energy. Imagine what can happen if we do everything this way: if you adopt a more optimistic outlook, the environment around you will change dramatically.

It is of utmost importance to reaffirm and persuade ourselves that the motivation for our actions is well-being, not obligation or duty. Before starting the exercise, we can even affirm it out loud numerous times before doing it.

For example, be sure to remember to say out loud things like "I want to swim," "I really like it," and "I feel fantastic." This can help you feel more satisfied and proud of yourself, as well as boost your health and fitness. Insist that you say "I want to swim" rather than "I have to swim". It is important to do this frequently to reinforce this uplifting feeling of personal development. This way, every time we start to feel unmotivated to do a certain activity that requires us to leave the couch or our comfort zone, we can bring to mind the fact that it is beneficial to us, how good we feel while doing it, and how, at the end of the day, we feel proud and satisfied with the effort we have made.

This has nothing to do with parachuting out of an airplane. Or is it? I'm talking about being brave enough to try new things and to accept the feelings of insecurity and uncertainty that come with venturing into unknown territory. I'm talking about making an effort to modify one's behavior and take an alternative route. We may "fail" because we are new to that habitat, or we may find something different that opens our eyes and gives us what we have been looking for for so long and what we needed most.

If you manage to find your rhythm, you'll find that becoming a better version of yourself is not only not scary, but one of the most exciting and satisfying things you can do in your life.

To be able to propose something and carry it out is to be able to materialize your ideas in the physical world. In this way, the intangible becomes real. It is a miracle. And life itself is a magical experience.

THE BEAUTY OF NONINTERPRETATION

It is inevitable, or rather, it is almost impossible, for us not to judge something when we see someone else's actions or are told a story about something that has just happened. We may judge it as good, right, wrong or horrible, but it almost never manages to pass us by. It is necessary for us to express our opinion. It's how we state our ideals and stand up for who we are, how we empathize with others or differentiate ourselves and how we express ourselves. And you're not wrong at all. But here comes the curious thing: when we create something good, that is, when we establish in our mind that a fact or a concept is correct, or that achieving a certain thing is the ideal, without wanting it, we are also creating something bad, because we give life to its opposite. It is very interesting to reflect on this. To put it another way, the fact that we have not yet achieved the positive goal we have set for ourselves is a drawback. For example, if we intended to finish our degree (something positive) but were unable to do so (something negative) due to unforeseen circumstances, such as our father becoming ill and we had to start working before we could do so, we would have negative emotions. Since what was supposed to make us feel good didn't come true or we didn't get it, we are not in a good mood. Unconsciously, we have trained our mind with the concept that it is unethical for us to get the opposite of what we wanted or not get the excellent thing we wanted. This has led us to believe that it is bad for us to have either of these outcomes. It is quite common to hear people say things like, "I didn't get that job I wanted," "I'm thirty years old and I'm not married yet," "I wanted to have had children before I was thirty-five," and other similar statements.

Clearly, these are truths that anyone would find disturbing or would prefer to ignore for the time being. There are also facts that are undoubtedly perverse and there is no other way of looking at them, such as crimes, homicides, sexual assaults and a long list of other examples. That is indisputable. But what really matters to us in this context are the realities of our daily existence.

Since we must confront the human mental conditioning that has been ingrained in us for centuries, it will be necessary to be acutely aware of our unconscious reactions in order to successfully apply the concept of neutral interpretation, even though its explanation is simple and its application challenging.

A neutral interpretation implies keeping one's own personality and sense of judgment under control in order to recognize that something is neither positive nor negative, but simply IS. Believe me when I tell you that simply to consider achieving this is already a positive evolution. It involves distancing oneself from the mind and the deceptions it can produce, as well as preventing the mind from forming judgments that lead us in the wrong direction or bring us no benefit.

For example, if I were driving on the road and someone crossed in front of me in a dangerous manner, I would sound my horn to give him an audible warning. If he then suddenly changes lanes and brakes, comes up to me and yells at me, insults me or makes aggressive hand gestures, I might follow his energetic flow and yell and insult him as well, making me an accomplice to his bad behavior and paying, at least forcefully, the consequences of his mistakes. Since I am not able to give my full attention to the road while I am angry, I am increasing the likelihood that I will be the one to cause an accident. This could end up being an even worse problem.

However, we can also simply take a deep breath, smile and make a gesture that expresses our regret for what happened, even if it was not even our fault, and continue on our way without further problems. In this way, we would prevent their negative energy from affecting and contaminating us and we could continue on our way without being harmed, maintaining the purity of our vibration. If you do not allow something to affect you, then it cannot. According to a well-known proverb, "he does not offend who wants to, but he who can". Therefore, you should not give a situation the opportunity to upset you. It is not about adopting a defensive posture, but counterattacking positively. It is about accepting and letting go of attachments. Acknowledge that the behavior doesn't make sense and put it back where it came from.

The problem is not ours until the moment we decide to take responsibility for it by responding negatively. It is not necessary to react, but to act, which implies accepting what happens and letting it pass or ignoring it. However, there are situations in which it is not even necessary to act.

None of this has anything to do with humiliating oneself or allowing oneself to be mistreated by another person. In real life, there is almost never an absolute right or wrong answer; instead, there is an almost infinite variety of shades of gray.

Keep this in mind: the next time you are overcome with hatred or resentment over someone's discourteous behavior or abuse, take a moment to reflect on whether it is worth wasting an entire day being angry or resentful just because someone wasted a minute of your time with discourteous words, intentions or manners.

Exercise:

Simply remove yourself from the situation if you are being tormented by negative energies, if you are subject to severe criticism or if you feel that your emotional or energetic balance is in danger. Do not interpret it, do not accuse it, and do not judge it in any way, regardless of whether it is feasible to walk away or not. Focus your attention on your breath and become aware of your body. You have the ability to say to yourself things like, "You are not mine, you don't belong to me and I don't want you here."

Or you may simply say, "I won't get anywhere in the end!"

You can also say something like: "We appreciate your participation. You will be hearing from us in the near future."

You are the one who gives existence to everything you wish or do not wish to have in your life and you are also the one who brings it all to an end. Take advantage of your ideas and don't give them the opportunity that they can take advantage of you; believe me when I tell you that they will if they don't find anyone to steer the ship when they arrive. Use your ideas to your advantage.

THE KEY TO ATTRACTION

I will never tire of saying that we are creative beings because it is the truth. As mentioned in the chapter titled "High Frequency," our ideas serve as the raw material from which our dreams are built. We have the ability to take something that is intangible and ethereal and transform it into something that is solid, "real" and material that exists in the world. If we make the decision to study a career because we want to be, for example, a journalist, we will have to go to school for several years, study, take exams and finally get the degree. We are going to look for a job and, in the end, we are going to find ourselves working as journalists. We've made it. Something that was once just a concept in our heads has become a fact as a result of our actions.

The vast majority of us are completely unaware of the magnitude of this power. We were not shown it or taught how to use it when we were children. However, throughout our lives, there are moments when we realize that there is more that determines our lives than the results of random or chance events. You were reflecting on an old acquaintance you hadn't spoken to in a few weeks when, out of the blue, you get a phone call. Or you meet someone for the first time and the next day you run into them again somewhere else; or you're looking for a job and someone offers you a unique opportunity while you're having a conversation with them, etc. Synchronicity is the term Carl Jung used to describe what some people call chance or causality.

The word "yes" is communicated by the universe through the phenomenon of synchronicity. It is the way to know that you are spending your time with the right person, in the right place, at the right time. If you make the most of that opportunity, you will undoubtedly learn something important or be in a position to learn or help someone else in some way. When you find yourself wondering "how is this possible, what a coincidence!", then it is the perfect time to be fully attentive and sensitive to what is happening around you. Something extraordinary may be happening, such as an opportunity to advance professionally or emotionally, or even both.

Our subconscious regulates our existence. During our time here on Earth, we are exposed to a plethora of stimuli, experiences and memories, all of which contribute to the programming of our unconscious self. All of this knowledge contributes to the construction of a unique aspect of our identity, a personal perspective that determines how we respond, if at all, to the events of everyday life. This unconscious chain of instinctive impulses or reactions has a decisive impact on our view of the world and modifies the way we perceive things in our immediate environment.

If we had a difficult childhood, it is possible that we distrust someone who wants to open up to us or who treats us well. It is also possible that the opposite happens to us: at the slightest opportunity we see to trust someone, we do it blindly and without waiting for that trust to be generated naturally, which can cause the other person to get scared and run away, or that they take advantage of us and use us.

As has always been the case, an important part of our lives is totally controlled by the subconscious, but we are not aware of this fact. What if, on the contrary, we could build a happier and more optimistic version of ourselves by naturally influencing our subconscious? That's not impossible, but it will require work and dedication on your part, like virtually everything worthwhile in life.

It's not going to happen in the blink of an eye or overnight that we become the best version of ourselves. If we did, we wouldn't achieve much and, after a while, we'd probably start to get bored with it, at which point we'd go back to the old ways. Wine takes years to age. Time, communication, affection, mutual understanding and attention to detail are the pillars of a healthy relationship. It takes more than water and sunshine for a tree to be robust and lush; it also takes time and love. So, let's not have the expectation that we can fix all our behavioral or perceptual problems in a jiffy.

When I have a bad thought, or when something prompts me to focus on things that are unfair or do nothing for me, I like to remember a phrase I wrote some time ago that goes like this:

"There is no such thing as perfection. When you accept it, everything becomes perfect."

What should be flawless is not the physical environment in which we live, but our methods of viewing and valuing it. We all make mistakes and sometimes things happen in nature that, depending on our point of view, may seem extremely cruel and destructive. But how we see the world determines how we see it, not the other way around.

If you change the way you perceive the world, the world around you will also change.

Exercise:

If we want to achieve a large or long-term goal, it is very useful and crucial to create those smaller tasks or goals necessary to reach the final goal. Setting these smaller goals and tasks is the key to success. Together, we will make significant progress over time. To get somewhere, walking is the most efficient means of transportation. Learning and growing as an individual is a journey that is certainly enjoyable. A small percentage of people have the guts to undertake this journey to evolve in many facets of their lives.

The plan is to write on a piece of paper a big goal that you would like to achieve in the long term. Now define monthly goals that you need to achieve to reach them. Perfect. Now you know what tasks you need to do on a weekly or daily basis to get a little closer to your big goal every day. Go for it!

1. On the first blank page of your shiny new notebook, write down the title of an important goal you have set for yourself. Your ideal job, your life plan, your sports goals, your perfect house, your independence from monetary worries... now write, underneath that significant title, all the smaller goals or tasks that are necessary to reach your ultimate goal. Don't be sloppy with the details. You should now be aware that the goal you have set for yourself has significant value and that you will be grateful for it once you have achieved it. As you complete the small tasks listed in the notebook day by day, you will move closer to achieving your overall goal. Study, research, talk to people who already know or are succeeding at something similar and version what they did to succeed in order to find out and practice what they did to achieve it. If there is any point

where you feel you are not making progress, try new strategies and different ways to achieve it. The simple act of writing it down is the first step to turning it into a concrete plan that, over time, can become a reality.

2. Repeat daily, out loud, what you want to do, the reasons why you want to do it, and act and speak as if you have already achieved it. For example: "I have a two-story modular white house in the countryside. A beautiful vegetable garden and solar panels. I enjoy it very much and I sunbathe in the summer in the garden with my wife and children". Visualize yourself in that circumstance, having successfully completed your goal, and do it in detail. Imagine what you would wear, how you would talk, the house you would live in and, most importantly, how you would feel if all these things were reality. Write it all down and then read it out loud as if you already know it all. Without hesitation, with enthusiasm and determination. If you combine all these strategies, you can achieve anything you set your mind to. Feel the power of creativity flowing from within you as you practice gratitude for this whole development process. Becoming a magnet for whatever you wish to attract into your life can be achieved by following the steps described above.

If you have willpower and determination, you can achieve anything you set your mind to.

THE ABILITY TO THINK LESS AND FEEL MORE

Notice how the passage of time seems to fly by, how you come up with the finest jokes, how grateful and joyful you are, and how you share that positive energy and affection with everyone around you when you receive good news and celebrate it. In this busy schedule there is no room for the mind to intrude with its endless chatter and incessant noise of empty thoughts. We are so busy living in the here and now, in the present, or, in other words, thinking less and feeling more, that we have little time to think about the past or the future. And don't you think it would be amazing to spend the whole of your life, or at least most of it, in a state of bliss similar to this?

It is certainly a possibility if we focus our attention on the moments in our lives when we operate on "autopilot" and the moments when we have total control over what we are doing. If we allow ourselves to be distracted by things like thinking about our worries or problems, looking at our cell phone or television, our mind is working for us and we have very little control over its functioning. Our appreciation for reality diminishes and we fall into a cycle of apathy, indifference and, more seriously, a diminished capacity for original thought and productive effort.

If, on the other hand, we are completely absorbed in an activity, a sport, an exciting job or a meaningful conversation with another person, then we are living in the here and now; we are more SOUL than MIND; we are thinking less and feeling more. It is a form of meditation in action, because we stop the mind from polluting the moment with its usual interference and we unleash our passion and creativity. This is how I choose to see things and it is the perspective that has helped me the most to direct my attention and my efforts towards living in the here and now, which is where everything takes place.

You can heal your soul by dedicating part of your energy to the cultivation of your mind. When we become aware that thoughts arise spontaneously in our head, without reason or trigger, and that many times those thoughts do not bring us anything or lead us to act or react in a negative way, we have taken the first step towards awareness. We are feeling. At this point, our heart leads our mind. When we have that aha! moment and realize that our unconscious mind does not represent who we are, but our conscious mind does, we have entered the magical realm. It is because of our conscious mind that we have choice. Being conscious is how we arrive at the best choices, when we mix reason and experience, thoughts and feelings, mind and soul. If everything was governed by instinct and not by consciousness, we would still be animals and would be forced to kill ourselves to stay alive.

Possibly, there are times when we cannot choose what to think about because the plate is already set before us. However, we can choose what to "feed", which means that we can choose which thoughts to pay attention to, which ones are worth developing and which ones require us to spend time on them that we will never get back.

Let's look at it from this perspective: Something that is not good for me, something that may not have even happened, a fear or a worry I have is going through my head right now. When we imagine something, the tremendous power of our mind makes it seem like it is actually happening. Our body puts every cell to work on that concept and all emotion, whether positive or bad, floods and controls us. The body is flooded with hormones that are created as a result of the emotions and, as a result, we lose awareness of what we are thinking and go into a feedback loop. Don't let that happen. You are free to end the process whenever you want. Because once an emotion has come into our being, logical reasoning fades away. Most of the time, we are emotional animals rather than rational animals.

Consider some of the unfavorable feelings that have been responsible for so much devastation on the planet: Envy, religious fanaticism, power, abuse and control, greed: all these things carry no good part and consume to the core the person who feels them.

Exercise:

When we have a thought that knocks at our door and does not make us happy, let us not worry, let us not feel, let us not give it value or meaning and let us not pay more attention to it than absolutely necessary. As it came, let it pass. Instead, let's focus on something else. To this point, throughout this book we have discussed various strategies to help you focus your mind on the here and now, and I believe that you now possess the necessary tools to begin to achieve this goal. It can all be summarized as follows: when a bad unconscious idea enters your mind, immediately replace it with a positive conscious thought. If you have negative thoughts, counteract them by taking positive actions. In other words, do not let yourself be carried along on your mind's journey, but rather direct it in the direction you want it to go. Use the techniques described in the previous chapters, such as touching the wall and feeling how it feels, touching your body and seeing how it feels, touching your clothes and seeing how they feel, focusing on your breathing, singing, humming, talking out loud, saying "I don't mind, thank you and good day," exercising, and writing in your power notebook "nothing bad stays with me." And then, as fast as you can process the information, it will disappear. You can accomplish this goal in several different ways; choose the approach that most appeals to you, the one that feels most natural to you, or the one that makes the most sense to you.

These strategies for living in the here and now are by no means exhaustive, nor are they the only ones that can be employed. There are probably many more and, as you go along, you may even find or come up with some new ones. The approaches shared in this book are the ones that worked for me and continue to be beneficial to me today. I sincerely hope they lighten some of your load and make it possible for you to soar more easily.

I thank you for being present at this moment.

CONCLUSION

Your inner journey of self-improvement and development may have just begun, or you may have been on it for some time, but the journey through this book has been successfully completed.

One of the many things that make life so beautiful is the ability to nourish ourselves from our surroundings to grow and develop on different levels. When we feel that something is bothering us, having the ability to go within can offer us a greater understanding of how our feelings, health, mind and soul work.

If we feed our minds with nourishing and uplifting thoughts, we will find that doing so has great effects on our lives. Our energy levels and willpower, as well as our concentration and mood, will experience significant improvements. We will also sleep better and, as a result, have a wonderful day, leading to the creation of a cycle of well-being that will greatly improve the quality of our existence.

Similarly, if we strive to be selective about the thoughts we pay attention to and ensure that only those that bring something beneficial to our lives continue to flourish, our mood will be calmer and free of worry and anxiety. We will be able to perform more effectively at work, our judgment will increase, we will have a more optimistic outlook and a host of other benefits.

We should not blame ourselves for what we think unconsciously; rather, we should accept responsibility for what we feel, for this requires more participation on our part than what we think unconsciously. A thought may appear spontaneously, but by giving it our full attention, we give it the opportunity to grow in power and strength. Make a proper decision about the aspects of yourself that you want to develop.

Similarly, our soul requires the necessary amount of "nourishment". The soul will feel at ease, happy and grateful if we take care of our mind in various ways and can call upon it at times when our mind "betrays" us. When we are able to immerse ourselves completely in the now without being diverted by anything else, we can access our soul, which is the place within us where everything is perfect, where there are no problems, no stress and no pain.

Feeling comes from the soul, while thinking comes from the mind. If we make the decision to entertain and cultivate only happy thoughts, the soul will provide us with sensations and feelings of happiness and general well-being. It may not be as easy as it seems to put it into practice, but like everything worthwhile in life, you have to put a minimum of effort into something important to achieve, nurture and maintain it. Once you understand your true power, every stage of your life will present you with opportunities to grow and enjoy abundance. Don't miss the opportunity to improve the quality of your life.

When you feel stressed or anxious, or when you think too much, refocus on your body and remember to breathe slowly and deeply. The same energy that makes you angry or stressed is also the energy that can help you relax and feel better. You just need to practice the skills necessary to control it and use it to your advantage.

All you need you already have it within you.

Thank you for deciding to read my book

I truly hope that the journey through the pages of this book has been enjoyable for you and that the lessons and motivation you have gained from reading my experiences will help you on your own path to personal development, mental health and happiness.

Help me to help

The most helpful thing you could do for me would be to write a positive review or rating of my book on the website where you got it. It won't take you more than a few seconds, but it would mean a lot to me.

If you value my work positively, it can reach more people and thus have a positive effect on their lives, health and well-being.

I hope your travels are filled with joy and that you find serenity and abundance.
Jun Sano

www.ingramcontent.com/pod-product-compliance
Lightning Source LLC
Chambersburg PA
CBHW050250010526
44107CB00003B/265